Fishing and Flying
A Homage to Terence Horsley

Drew Jamieson

With illustrations by C.F. Tunnicliffe OBE, RA. (1901-1979)

Drew Jamieson

ISBN: 9798609286987
Imprint: Independently published

By the same Author

The Ochil Hills: A Special Place (2018)
Where the Wild Trout Swim (2018)
Where the Wild Salmon Run (2018)
A Scottish Angler's Companions (2018)
Trout from Scottish Reservoirs (2019)
The Trout Reservoirs of Lothian (2019)
Scotland's Wild Salmon (2019)

Independently published
Available on Amazon

Front Cover and Title Page:
Reproduced by kind permission of The Estate of C.F. Tunnicliffe OBE, RA.

DEDICATION

To Morny, my wife and soul-mate,
through the ups and downs of a pilot's life and the ripples
of "Moon River".

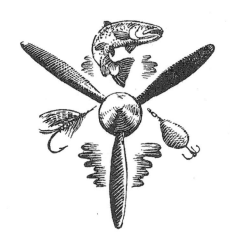

FLIGHT

Far beneath me ant-size children
Glimpse our contrails cross the sky
But cannot see the rainbow
Brilliant, dazzling to the eye.

The anvil cloud and lightning flashes
The rainbow arcs of an autumn day
Are tapestries in our cathedral
Which raise our eyes and make us pray

That the line we etch across the sky
Be bold and straight and true
And that we never forget, in age,
That such was the road we knew.

Adapted from
"The Aviator" by Skip Hatter
and "Flight" by John Williams

CONTENTS

ACKNOWLEDGMENTS

No man is an island - and certainly not a pilot, an angler or a writer. Along the way I have had support and encouragement from fellow pilots, ghillies, scientists, writers and fellow anglers.

The drawings are by Charles F. Tunnicliffe, as printed in Terence Horsley's original edition of *Fishing and Flying* published in 1947. They are re-printed by kind permission of The Estate of C.F. Tunnicliffe OBE, RA.

Photo credits: Rod Rennet p. viii; South Uist AC p. 94. Internet: Creative Commons p.23, p.53. Many of the photographs of aircraft were taken by fellow-pilots, identity unknown. My thanks to them. Other photos and sketches by the author. Maps and satellite images are by Google Earth and Apple Maps where credited.

My special thanks goes to Morny, my wife and fellow-traveller, for her patient proof-reading and for putting up with life with a pilot, an angler, a writer and a Pict. Any remaining errors are all mine.

FOREWORD

Terence Horsley has been part of Finavon for as long as I can remember. When I took over ownership of the Finavon Castle Fishings, he was already an established legend and a benign spirit.

Lieutenant Commander Terence Beresford Horsley RN was a keen sportsman and glider pilot who flew Swordfish and other aircraft with the Fleet Air Arm during the Second World War. He wrote articles under the nom-de-plume of "Stringbag" and published a series of fascinating books on naval air power, gliding, shooting, fishing and flying. Perhaps his most famous is his *Fishing and Flying*, published in 1947.

Horsley was a tenant of Finavon in 1941. Based at Royal Naval Air Station Arbroath - HMS Condor - he flew over the river regularly on his way back to base to check its condition and water level before coming to fish later. There is a stone in the middle of the river, shaped like the moulded seat of an aircraft, where Horsley is reputed to have sat awaiting the 'sea trout hour'. His book make much reference to what he called his 'Little River', based upon his experiences at Finavon and we consider Terence Horsley to be part of the Finavon family.

I have known the author of this new version for many years and I am delighted to see the old title *Fishing and Flying* being resurrected in a new form. It must of course be a very different book, relating experiences of flying and fishing a generation after Horsley. The technology and science of flying has progressed rapidly since Horsley's day. Fishing less so - but change it must. With a changing climate some of it will be forced upon us.

Tony Andrews,
Finavon Castle Fishings,
South Esk,
Angus.

"Fishing and Flying": the two passions of Terence Horsley

TERENCE HORSLEY

I first met Terence Horsley in the pages of his classic book, *Fishing and Flying,* published in 1947. From the ecstasies of tumbling a high-performance aircraft through the clouds, corries and passes of the Cairngorms at 360 mph, to the quiet magic of fishing the night estuary for sea trout, Horsley had me in thrall, leading me intensely through his two contrasting worlds of flying and fishing.

I met Horsley again, flying my Chipmunk trainer in 1960. A navigation exercise crossed the South Esk, where Horsley had fished and the runways of HMS Condor from where he flew, lay on the coast near Arbroath.

I was reminded of him again in the 1970s, flying my Canberra bomber across the Cairngorm mountains on my way to RAF Lossiemouth on the Moray coast.

Perhaps I came closest to him, in later life, while night-fishing for sea trout on his favourite 'Little River' - the South Esk.

Terence Horsley died in gliding accident at Bradwell Edge, in Derbyshire on April 24, 1949 at the age of 45. His obituary, in *The Aeroplane* of 13 May 1949 starts with Benjamin Franklin's quote:

> *They that can sacrifice essential liberty*
> *For a little temporary safety*
> *Deserve neither liberty nor safety.*

NURSERY STREAMS

Young salmon emerge from their sheltering gravel into the wonderful yet dangerous world of the nursery stream. For the first part of their life they are totally dependent upon the attached yolk-sac for their food and survival. As they grow through fry and parr they have to learn to survive and to imprint themselves with the heritage of their native stream.

So the young aviator has to learn to fly and survive and to imprint himself with the heritage of his profession.

1. LEARNING TO FISH

"I think however that the keenest anglers are born and not made: that the passion is latent in them from the beginning, and is revealed sooner or later according to opportunity."

Grey of Fallodon. *"Fly Fishing"*.

I was born in Glasgow. The Allander Water and the Mugdock Reservoirs fascinated me with their clear water and the mystical rings produced by rising trout. The magic of fishing was born! Wartime Glasgow was a good place to get away from and at every opportunity we would migrate to the, then, rural village of Tullibody in Clackmannanshire. In 1949 we moved there permanently and I learned to fish.

The Delph ponds at Tullibody were full of wildlife but it was the fish that were the major fascination in those days. Sticklebacks, or 'baggie minnins' were the main quarry to start with. Caught with a small worm tied onto a piece of thread and kept in a jam, or 'jeely', jar. They had their own hierarchy. The colourful males in full spawning dress were stunning. With an electric blue-green back and scarlet chest - known to us as 'rid-breesters' - they were a popular quarry but the big trophies were the pregnant females, green and silver in colour, and several times the size of the males. The largest got the acclaim as 'sousters' and would almost fill a jam jar on their own and earned bragging rights among the young anglers. Peter Masting was my fishing companion in those days. Eventually we caught a perch and there were rumours of even bigger fish. Fearsome pike were supposed to lie in wait for unwary boys but, although we were there almost every day in summer, we never saw any evidence of them. No dead bodies, no disappearing ducklings, no tell-tale swirl of water from the shallows - nothing. One autumn we saw a pair of trout, brown trout, big trout. Perhaps this pair had been introduced by someone. Perhaps each autumn they came to the inflow pipe to savour the sweet water which reminded them of their youth and the urges to run upstream to spawn - but could not do so. But their size and mystery cast a spell which set me off on the next leg of my angler's quest - the pursuit of wild trout.

With growing confidence we explored the Ochil Hills. Alex Scott and I fished the Gannel Burn, above Tillicoultry on many days before either of us caught our first trout. Setting off in the early morning with very basic kit - Alex's recycled aerial from a WW2 tank and my remaining six feet of an old 9-foot greenheart rod - we would fish the accessible pools on the Tillicoultry Burn and then turn right, up the Gannel, leap-frogging each other from pool to pool, trying to be polite about sharing the most likely bits but secretly competing to catch the most – or any - trout.

It was a long, but great, apprenticeship of exhilarating days in the rain or the sun, when the excuses for failure were many – too cold, too bright, water too low! But eventually we gained the knowledge - which pools held the biggest trout; dull weather was best; a little colour in the water was helpful; when the trout fed – and empty baskets became less frequent. The Daiglen had good fishing pools. The Burn of Sorrow could be reached over the watershed from the Gannel.

Alex on the Gannel

One memorable day we crossed the watershed at Maddy Moss and like 'stout Cortez' viewing the Pacific – we looked down the valley of the Brioch, to the great lowland of Strathearn and the vast rampart of the Grampian Mountains beyond. Our horizons had suddenly exploded. Down the Brioch we fished and up the Grodwell. Another long summer's day of an east wind and clear blue sky we got, not exactly lost, but 'temporarily unsure of our position!' We had fished up the Gannel and down the Brioch, crossed the ridge to fish down the Frandy and then set off for home - only to find ourselves in Glen Sherup. It was a long hungry hike back to Tillicoultry, but Leah Scott's banana sponge and fresh scones refuelled me for my cycle back to Tullibody.

The River Devon was our next adventure, a delightful trout stream celebrated by Thomas Tod Stoddart, the 19th century angler-explorer, who visited the river in 1834. He wrote: "A portion of the valley through which the Devon or Dovan flows has been termed the Arcadia of Scotland. The scenery it presents is unquestionably of a very picturesque description." When I left Tullibody it was more than 40 years before I cast a line in the Devon again but little snapshots of early days on the Devon always come back to mind:

• There was a riffle below the bridge at Dollar. It was a thin, fast, 'popply' run. In the quiet dusk of an April evening it reflected the apple-green afterglow behind the Ochil Hills. Drifting a team of small wet flies downstream produced a "tap-tap-tap" and "knock-knock-knock" of numerous small trout and salmon parr, giving the sensation of a river alive and teeming with fish.

• There was a run between Blairingone and Dollar, surrounded by trees, but accessible from the south side. It is not a deep run and most times it is unoccupied. But in the early morning of the stone-fly season it is occupied by one or more large trout. They lie barely covered and a crafty angler floating a big fat female stone-fly can be rewarded with an explosive, slashing rise and a firm take of a quality wild trout. It happens once in a lifetime but is never forgotten.

• There was a glide below the bridge at Dunning Glen. It was a deep glide and a fast glide and difficult to see what lay within. But on a bright May morning when the water was clear and the trout were 'on the fin', there was a goodly trout hovering just off the current and within casting distance of a young angler. As the fly floated down the trout flexed its pectoral fins, tilted its nose towards the surface and sucked it in. It weighed a mere 8 oz. but has never been forgotten.

Learning to catch salmon came much later.

2. LEARNING TO FLY

"The Chipmunk aircraft bounced across the grass of Perth Airfield. The Gypsy Major engine strained at full throttle, making every horse-power count. Bounce, bounce, bounce - suddenly smoothness. We are flying. It is that magic moment when gravity falls away and the weight of the aircraft, one excited student and his, less-excited, instructor, are carried aloft by the movement of the air across a cambered wing, with no obvious means of support."

There are a certain number of 'firsts' in any young man's life. His first trout - done!. His first salmon - still in the future! His first take-off in the front seat of a Chipmunk has to be up there with the best. All one's life one has been anchored to the ground. For much of one's life one has looked skywards and dreamed of being like a bird. In an instant it has happened and, even with the eventual knowledge of aerodynamics, it is still, and always will be, a magical experience.

"Mischievous laughing boys, who grew to quick manhood....."

Together with some twenty other students I came to learn to fly. From council estates and tenement flats, from suburban bungalows and detached villas, young men converged on Scone. We walked from Perth railway station. We rode the A9 on old motorbikes, or even older cars. We came with the Corporal on the Squadron bus. From all parts of Scotland and further afield – England, Wales, Ireland, Nigeria, Norway and even Mauritius – we gravitated to Scone, as members Glasgow University Air Squadron, Royal Air Force Volunteer Reserve, to push the boundaries of our expertise, our comfort zones, our courage and our comradeship on a small windswept patch of grass, smooth enough to take off and land six Chipmunk aircraft. It was the stage on which we strutted our hour, full of sound and laughter signifying, not the 'nothing' of Shakespeare's prose, but a great up-welling of spirit, of comradeship, of new and far horizons.

Memories come back of freezing, winter mornings, dozy from sitting up beyond midnight learning checks, not compatible with the early-morning alertness needed for flying. There was probably only one winter and only two or three freezing mornings but they stick in the mind like honey and

8

taste as sweet. Walking across the tarmac from the Airwork Mess to the Flight Hut with frost on the ground, lungs sucking in icy air and getting rid of the fug of the night before. Breakfast was always a cooked breakfast - bacon, eggs, sausage, beans and fried bread - would either kill or cure a hangover. A standard motto was: 'if you were going to be sick in the aircraft you had better have something to be sick with'.

Chipmunks

Far away to the north, the Grampians are covered in snow. Our skiing friends will be up at Glenshee. Given a few solo slots we might go and show the flag and buzz the ski slopes. Otherwise, it is a perfect day. Clear polar air drifting down from the north, visibility unlimited, a few clouds for reference. No turbulence. We can cope with any exercises today. Today may be 'bingo' day, perhaps some staff continuation training. We can go as passengers and perhaps get some tail-chases and formation flying. Long before our own training reaches these giddy heights our appetites are whetted. Anything to get that favoured spare seat with our instructor and to follow the five aircraft around the sky in a tail chase. Sergeant Cooper gets the coke alight before freezing students arrive and huddle around the stove awaiting the flying programme's first wave – struggling with checks and procedures, nervous of instructors, fearful of failure. From the threshold of the runway I see again the stumbling approaches of early failures - rocking wings, over-correcting, sweating blood. Many relieved they were 'chopped' before they threw in the towel.

We learned our basic exercises - Straight and Level, Medium Turns, Stalling and Spinning. We progressed to Aerobatics, Navigation, Instrument Flying, Formation and, even, a little bit of Night Flying. One Summer Camp was at RAF Horsham St Faiths outside Norwich in Norfolk. This was close to RAF Coltishall, the base for the RAF's newest fighter - the English Electric Lightning armed with Firestreak missiles. We also paid a visit to the USAF base at Sculthorpe, near Fakenham. In 1961, that part of Norfolk still resonated with the history of the USAAF Eighth Air force which had so many wartime stations in that area. I joined the Royal Air Force in 1963.

* * * * *

Just as the young salmon after two years or so in the sheltered waters of its nursery stream has to run a gauntlet of risks to make it to the wide ocean, so the aviator, carefully nurtured in the quiet life of a light aircraft must enter into the world and risks of jet flying.

In 1964 I found myself in Nottinghamshire learning to fly jets. Not very fast jets but the Jet Provost Mk 4 was faster than a Chipmunk. After the nimble Chipmunk, the Jet Provost was a bit of a truck to fly. Yes, it was jet-powered but acceleration was slow, controls were heavy, the instrument panel seemed a long way away. The side-by-side seating made the cockpit seem very wide and I felt detached from the aeroplane, compared to the snug fit of the tandem cockpit and the view out both sides of the cockpit in the 'Chippie'

One particular learning incident comes to mind when I was well into the Jet Provost course.

"I rejoined the circuit for a 'run-in-and-break' and turned 'downwind' in the approved manner with the airbrakes OUT, waiting for the airspeed to reduce below 180 knots in order to lower the undercarriage. I waited and waited and the speed did not reduce below an indicated 200 knots. The controls started to feel sloppy and eventually I felt the buffet of an approaching stall. I flicked in the airbrakes and increased the power to cruise setting and the aircraft stabilised. I called Tower and alerted them to my perceived problem - an inaccurate Air Speed Indicator (ASI). A shepherd aircraft was vectored on to me and followed me round the circuit calling out our collective airspeeds. My own Air Speed Indicator started to read correctly again half-way round the circuit when my airspeed increased back above 200 knots but my shepherd talked me all the way down to touchdown. There were raised eyebrows and a degree of disbelief as I filled in my Incident Report but the suspect Air Speed Indicator was taken out and sent off for tests. I forgot all about it until some months later, I was summoned to the Flight Commander's office to be advised that, after exhaustive tests, the engineers had managed to replicate the fault in the Air Speed Indicator. They had got it to stick at 200 knots on deceleration. *"I learned about technology from that!"*

* * * *

After gaining my 'Wings' on the Jet Provost, I went to Anglesey for advanced training on the Folland Gnat T Mk 1. The Gnat was a wonderful, if slightly dangerous, aeroplane. It was small, tiny even. You did not get into it, so much as put it on, like a slipper. It fitted around you, bottom scraping the ground, feet in the nose with a beautiful big bubble canopy providing 360 degree vision.

It was a fast little beast - the Formula One of the air. You opened the throttle and 'whooshed' down the runway and were airborne before you knew it. It was very sensitive on the hydraulic controls requiring twitchy fingers - finger and thumb stuff - compared to the Jet Provost. It was the hydraulic system that provided any real challenge. The powered flying controls had a manual reversion which was quite tricky to master and if you had no hydraulics, your wheels and flaps might not work either.

The Folland Gnat

I enjoyed flying the Gnat once I had caught up with it. We used to low-fly on a one-way system up and down the valleys of the Snowdonia National Park, below the level of the A5 road! Abiding memories include a summer late-night sortie to Shawbury for a radar approach and becoming completely disoriented by the "leans", as the semi-circular canals in my ears picked up the wrong balance signals. I had to break off the approach and climb up above the mountains to get my bearings and stabilise my brain. Returning to base, I arrived at the top of the recovery TACAN dive still disoriented and very tired about 2 a.m. and was very pleased to see the runway lights of Valley.

* * * * *

From Valley, I went to Cambridgeshire to learn to fly the Canberra bomber. The Canberra was the RAF's first jet bomber, designed in the 1940s to replace the Lancaster and

Lincolns. It had first flown in 1949 and could still, in the 1960s, out-perform many more modern aircraft at high altitude. Many of its components were shared with the Lancaster but the Canberra could still fly high, fly long and fly fast.

Canberra B Mk. 2

My lasting memories of the course were that the Canberra was a big, heavy aeroplane compared to the diminutive and nimble Gnat that I had left. It had no powered flying controls and required a lot of muscle to make it do what you wanted it to do. This was especially so at high speed and particularly on asymmetric flight on one engine. The outlook from the cockpit, through the 'blister' canopy was poor, especially in the T4 trainer. I was quite short and had to have the seat raised as high as possible, just to see out. With the seat raised high, I could not reach the rudder pedals properly to control asymmetric flight. Tricky - but we got there in the end and passed out of the course as a Canberra pilot.

3. IMPRINTING FISHERMEN
An Angler's Heritage

The tall, rangy figure worked his way steadily up the Tweed to where I sat resting after lunch. Rhythmically, he cast his short line upstream, let it drift down a few feet, took a step forward and cast upstream again. His ten-foot greenheart rod seemed strangely out of place, but it put his horsehair line lightly on the water. I waved a greeting as he drew level, and he nodded in acknowledgement.

"What are they taking today?" I hailed. Silently, he waded across, water cascading from ancient wading stockings and squelching from battered iron-shod brogues. He held out his cast for inspection - three straggly-looking spiders dressed with long, soft hackles in black, red and dun. I pulled out my own fly wallet to search among the gaudy lures and winged wet-flies. He beat me to it and, from a faded pigskin wallet, pulled a cast of three similar spider patterns looking uncommonly like a Golden Plover Spider, Dotterel Spider and Partridge Spider, all whipped firmly on to silkworm gut of apparently vast diameter.

"You'll never catch anything with that leader," I suggested, passing him my reel of finest tippet. He smiled, arched an eyebrow knowingly, raised a silent hand to decline my offer, and then, as an answer, lifted the lid of his willow creel to reveal a basket of almost a dozen creditable trout, larger than I had seen all season from this part of the river. He smiled sympathetically at my amazement, slipped quietly back into the river and set off, casting upstream. I shook myself back to the present. The river was deserted. There were no puddles from dripping waders. The only fly wallet was my own, and across my lap lay an open volume - *The Practical Angler*, by W. C. Stewart, dated 1857.

"Do you never get lonely?" my wife asks from time to time when I return from one of my solo fishing trips. "Lonely?" I reply absent-mindedly, drifting off into the recollection of the day just past. I don't think I have ever yet given her an answer to that question, but perhaps one day she will understand how I have the pleasure of the company of that great band of anglers who have fished the waters before us.

I first made the acquaintance of Thomas Tod Stoddart up at St Mary's Loch, where he took me on one of his *Angler's Rambles*, of 1866. Down the Yarrow and up the Ettrick we fished, and on up the Megget Water and over to Loch Skene. He introduced me to Mrs Richardson - the redoubtable Tibby Shiels who kept the 'howff' of that name and entertained a motley band of eccentric angling guests who foregathered at the inn each season between 1828 and 1840. Now, when I fish in that part of Scotland, it is difficult not to hear the ribald laughter of Stoddart and his friend, James Hogg, the Ettrick Shepherd, drifting across St Mary's Loch on the day of May 4, 1833, when they boated 79 trout which scaled 36 lb.

I cannot fish the Clyde without seeing the young lad, with his 12-foot rod, his tin of worms and his wallet of small flies, who introduced me to that part of the river at Crawford. Young Henry Lamond went on to be secretary of the Loch Lomond Angling Improvement Association and eventually president of the Scottish Anglers' Association, but I first bumped into him in his book, *Days and Ways of a Scottish Angler,* published in 1932. Recalling his youthful days around the turn of the century, he invited me to join him on a trip up the Clyde from Crawford up beyond Elvanfoot one warm June day. Up through the Glespin pool he took me and on up the Stoneyburn and Blackbraes pools without success. He showed me where he used to get five-pounders from the Rowan Tree pool before the overhanging trees were cutback. With youthful energy, we went on up through the Newton pool below the Elvanfoot viaduct and on into the Daer valley where: "One would hardly believe without experiencing it for oneself the immense loneliness of this great basin in the hills, or realise the almost uncanny silence that prevailed." I wonder what he would think of the vast reservoir which now fills this valley?

I usually meet Terence Horsley when I fish the South Esk. In his book, *Fishing and Flying* of 1947, the roar of his Second World War aero-engine first shattered my peace as he skimmed over the treetops of the Finavon beat, looking for poachers and checking the level of the river to see if it was worth fishing that night. He almost flew into the trees one afternoon, so intent was he on looking for sea trout and salmon. Then the world would have been deprived of another beautiful angling book.

"Lonely?" I don't think so! Mind you, I have never actually seen any of my companions. I may have felt them from time to time and I am sure they have recognised me as they have passed me on the river-bank. It is not too difficult when up to your knees in water, fishing the 'gloaming rise', to feel the hair on the back of your neck tingle and sense the grey, shadowy shapes of that great host of anglers past, who taught us how to enjoy our fishing and left the sparkling waters signed with their story.

4. IMPRINTING PILOTS
An Aviator's Heritage

You drive past them without noticing them. A piece of rusty fence perhaps; a tumble of bricks; a farmer's large shed is all there is to see from the ground. But, from up aloft, an abandoned airfield is much different. Laid out like a chequerboard of broken runways, bits of taxiway, the odd hardstanding, surrounded by polygons of crops and pasture regained by the farmers after all the noise and activity of flying has passed into history.

To the airman they are many things. They usually make good landmarks for navigation - provided you know which ones they are and where they should be to start with. They provide comfort and reassurance. Flying around with a single engine of ancient design it is always useful to know where one might land if the said single engine stopped or played up. There might be fences across the runways now or large beasts might roam at will but at least there should be some reasonably flat area to scrape into 'in extremis'.

Errol disused airfield

But abandoned airfields are also the airman's heritage. Below his wing he sees not just old concrete and new fields but the flyers of yesterday, their adventures, their fears and challenges, successes and failures and the vital community who worked to keep their aircraft in the air. The flyers and their aircraft are all gone now, of course, but to stand in the middle of one of those old airfields is to see and hear and smell the dramas absorbed into the sacred soil. It does not take much imagination to hear again the whine of a propellor in fine-pitch and the growl of a Merlin engine straining for take-off or the welcome squeal of rubber at the end of a stressful mission.

Flying around Perth, our flying heritage was painted upon the ground beneath us. Marked on our flying charts as small blue dots surrounded by a blue circle and named in blue beside them lay the airfields which had long ago served their purpose - Errol, Tealing, Montrose, Edzell, Arbroath and even the seaplane base at Woodhaven, on the south side of the Tay estuary. They all have a story to tell.

Montrose became the first operational military aerodrome in the United Kingdom on 26 February 1913 when five aircraft of No 2 Squadron, Royal Flying Corps, arrived from Farnborough after completing the 450 mile (720 km) journey north in 13 days. This allowed aircraft to protect the Royal Navy bases at Rosyth, Cromarty and Scapa Flow. The First World War started on 28 July 1914 and, in August, No 2 Squadron moved to France. During the aerodrome's early days as a pilot training school it gained a reputation of - "a crash every day and a funeral every week". The military gravestones at the local cemetery bear witness to the numerous deaths of those learning to fly. Montrose is famous for its ghosts and has been described as possibly one of the most haunted places in Britain. Lieutenant Desmond Arthur was the original Montrose ghost. Killed in a flying accident on 27 May 1913, his spirit is said to have haunted the Officers' Mess. There have been many other unexplained sightings of apparitions in pilots' uniforms and phantom planes. In 2010, wartime music and speech was heard to come from a 70-year-old radio which was not powered in any way. RAF Montrose closed in 1952 and today is the location of the highly-acclaimed Montrose Air Station Heritage Centre.

Edzell was another good navigation feature with its two disused runways. An airfield was first established to the east of Edzell village during the First World War and was disbanded in 1919. During the 1930s it operated as a civilian airfield, but the outbreak of the Second World War saw its return to service in 1940, as RAF Edzell. During its active years it had connections with No 612 (County of Aberdeen) Squadron, Royal Auxiliary Air Force, usually based at Dyce. The airfield also served as an aircraft maintenance facility, and by the end of the war held some 800 aircraft in reserve. For some years after the war the airfield was still packed full of Lancaster and Lincoln bombers that had, reputedly, returned to the UK from one of the last bombing attacks on Germany. The aircraft had been diverted to Edzell because their bases on the east coast of England were covered in fog. Latterly, under lease to the United States Navy, the station hosted the 17th Space Surveillance Squadron operating a radar sensor for the USAF Spacetrack System, tracking enemy missile launches and low-altitude space surveillance until its final closure in 1997.

Arbroath was first constructed as a Fleet Air Arm base (HMS Condor) in 1938. It was opened on 19 June 1940 as a training base for naval aviators. A purpose-built 'aircraft carrier-sized' landing area was constructed on the airfield and was used to train aircrew in deck landing operations. Throughout the war years operational squadrons from aircraft carriers would take it in turn to spend rest periods while their ships were undergoing maintenance at Scottish ship repair facilities. Terence Horsley flew from here during the Second World War and many of his adventures in *Fishing and Flying* are based on his time in Arbroath. Flying stopped in 1954 and in 1971 the base became the home to 45 Commando Royal Marines.

Tealing just north of Dundee was visible from our Local Flying Area. It was opened in March 1942 to house No. 56 Operational Training Unit (OTU) equipped with Hawker Hurricane, Miles Master and Westland Lysander aircraft. The number of pilots training at the unit reached a peak of 150 on 1943. It has a special claim to fame. Amid a local news blackout on 20 May 1942, Vyacheslav Molotov, Russian Foreign Minister, landed in secret. He arrived to meet with Sir Winston Churchill at Chequers and signed the Anglo-Soviet Treaty on 26 May. At a later stage, Tealing housed No. 9 (Pilots) Advanced Flying Unit, flying Miles Masters and Harvards and used Errol as a satellite landing ground.

Errol was located in the middle of our Local Flying Area on the Carse of Gowrie. Its three runways were highly visible from the air and made an ideal target for Practice Forced Landings - much to the disturbance of the good people on the ground. Errol opened in January 1943 and was occupied by No. 305 Ferry Training Unit. This was a special training and conversion unit for the Soviet crews receiving deliveries of Armstrong Whitworth Albemarle bombers to take back to Russia to fight on the Eastern Front. This joint operation continued until April 1944 and the military role of the airfield ended in 1948. As an RAF station it originally featured a control tower and 6 hangars but most of the buildings around the airfield were derelict or in a state of poor repair.

So much for the infrastructure and the history - but what of the people - the young pilots, navigators and ground crew disrupted from family, friends and familiar surroundings and sent to remote airfields with discomfort, injury or death an ever-present shadow. When you stand in the middle of an abandoned airfield you can feel and hear its past.

"The growl of Merlins, the squeal of rubber…"

In its flat centre you see the horizon-wide, open sky into which the aircrew launched. The silence is palpable. Wind whispers in the weeds breaking up the runways. A lark stutters somewhere overhead. But, in their prime, these fields were alive with aircraft and people, a cacophony of noise and activity, reverberating to aircraft engine, slipstreams, vehicles and young voices. Voices full of fear, relief, nerves, courage and determination. Their stories echo down the years. Nowhere does the network of disused airfields fire the imagination than in East Anglia. Nowhere resonates with the ghosts of the airmen past, than Norfolk and Suffolk. A Summer Camp took me to Norfolk, flying over the abandoned airfields of the American 8th Army Air Force. It is not a place for fertile imaginations.

Ghosts Over Norfolk

There is one 'Theory of Time', which says that historic events exist in a series of circles, which may revolve in different directions and at different speeds but which, every so often, coincide and 'Times Past' surface in the 'Present'. I am not saying that I fully adhere to that theory but, every so often, some strange combination of circumstances encourages me to re-visit it. It may be difficult to separate fact from fiction but both as a fisher and as a flyer I can be afflicted.

"I orbit left, 360 degrees, carrying out my 'lookout', before I spin my Chipmunk. The sky is all clear below. It is 1961. I am on Summer Camp at Horsham St Faiths, working towards my Preliminary Flying Badge – the Volunteer Reserve 'Wings'. I am authorised for a solo spinning exercise.

I clear the circuit for the local flying area via Rackheath, one of the many disused airfields in the area. I climb south, navigating by other disused airfields - Seething, Hardwick and Thorpe Abbotts. At the very south of our Local Flying Area I am at 6500 feet, or Flight Level 65, carrying out my checks before spinning - Height, Airframe, Security, Engine - are all OK. Location? I am overhead the disused airfield of Thorpe Abbots, some twenty miles south of Norwich. Lookout - Left-hand orbit completed. Orbit right 360 degrees. Clear all round. Clear below. No other aircraft in the sky. Checks complete, I close the throttle, keep straight, ball in the middle. Raise the nose as the speed drops off. No trimming below 70 knots. Into the buffet – control column smoothly and centrally back, full right rudder and I am spinning - yawing right, rolling right, nose just below the horizon. One turn, two turns, three turns. As the nose rotates, the horizon merges into Norfolk's summer haze. Time to recover – full left rudder, pause, stick coming centrally forward....but it doesn't......... The rotation increases, the nose comes up, the spin flattens and winds up, faster, faster......... The world goes gray, then black.

"Letter D on a big yellow background......"

"I see the big tail fin first, with the letter "D" on a square yellow background and the serial number 23393 beneath it. The rest of the big four-prop is muted green with the letter 'Y' clear on its aft fuselage. It cuts across my nose from right to left. *'Just a-Snappin'* is the name on the nose. The insignia is the United States 8th Army Air Force.

Major Jack Kidd leads the raid from the co-pilot's seat, earphones squashing his peaked service cap. Ev Blakely is at the controls. Jim Douglass, bombardier, is in the nose with Ed Forkner, radio operator, down the back. The gunners are settling in. Monroe Thornton and Bill McClelland are in the top and ball turrets. Lester Saunders and Ed Yevich man the waist guns and Charlie Via the usual co-pilot, sits in the tail as formation control officer in this lead crew and covers the tail. Lieutenant Harry Crosby, lead navigator for the raid and the future author of *On a Wing and a Prayer* is in the nose. Saunders, Nordstrom and Forkner would not survive the war.

Heavily laden with its 6000 lb bomb load, the B17 Flying Fortress struggles for height at 300 feet per minute. All four engines at full-power, claw into the smooth air at 150 miles per hour, throwing it back, smashed and twisted, in the slipstream. It orbits slowly in the climb, its airfield radio beacon 15 degrees off centre, maintaining a single needle's width on the rate of turn indicator.

There are other B17s behind '*Just a-Snappin*'. Five more of the 418th Bombardment Squadron are airborne and climbing. Fifteen more from the 349th and 350th are lined up on the runway and the perimeter track. The 100th Bomber Group of the United States 8th Army Air Force (8AAF) – 'The Bloody Hundredth' – is on a mission. I hitch a ride with them for a while.

By noon, twenty-one B17s of the Bloody 100th are at 5000 feet, formed up in seven vics in defensive formation. The 350th is high squadron, the 418th is middle and the 349th is low. They head north-east. From Framlingham and Horsham airfields the 390th and the 95th Bomber Groups are also airborne. Eighteen minutes later at 9000 feet the three groups join up over Lowestoft. By 1330 hrs the Flying Fortresses of the 3rd Air Division are in place. Over the Wash they assemble with the B24 Liberators of the 2nd Air Division and the B17s of the 1st Air Division. The 2nd and 3rd Divisions head north-east out over the North Sea. The 1st Air Division heads directly east over Holland. Bremen is the target. It is 8 October 1943. I leave them to their mission."

My spin stops at 3000 feet. Vision returns. I centralize the rudder and ease back on the control column. Directly below the nose are the broken remains of the three intersecting runways of Thorpe Abbotts. Among the green and yellow fields are the tracings of taxiways and hard standings and a well-preserved control tower.

"Ev Blakely, Jack Kidd and the crew of *'Just a-Snappin'* are hit hard by flak over Bremen, spin out of control and only superb flying saves them from crashing. With the two starboard engines knocked out and their props feathered they come home at low altitude with 1200 shell holes. On the way home they are attacked repeatedly by Luftwaffe fighters and shoot down ten of them. Saunders is dying. Yevitch, Forkner, McClelland, Via and Douglass are injured. Rather than ditch in the North Sea they struggle to landfall and crash land at the dummy airfield of RAF Ludham on the Norfolk coast. They hit the only tree on the airfield and write off *'Just a-Snappin'* Seven of the twenty-one B17s of the Bloody 100th do not return that day. Seventy-two crewmen die."

I pull out of the dive and return to base, navigating home by the ghosts of the US 8th Army Air Force:

- Bishops Thorpe (100th Bombardment Group) B17s;
- Hardwick (93rd Bombardment Group) B24s;
- Seething (448th Bombardment Group) B24s;
- Rackheath (467th Bombardment Group) B24s;
- Horsham St Faiths (458th Bombardment Group) B24s.

On every disused airfield, on every broken hard-standing and every derelict taxiway sit the giant ghosts of the B17s and B24s. Grey crosses on the giant cemetery of the US Eighth Army Air Force.

Born of the sun, they travelled a short while toward the sun
And left the vivid air signed with their honour.

Stephen Spender

5. ABOVE THE CLOUDS

Like the salmon, the aviator has to navigate the world and get himself home again. In early years he relied upon the sun, stars, magnetic compass and timepiece. Then came the magic of radio waves, the radio compass and radio direction finding (RDF). Then there was GEE and radar and distance measuring equipment (DME) and LORAN and Decca Navigator and TACAN - and now we can rely on satellite navigation systems (GPS and SATNAV). But in the early days we had the same challenges as salmon but without their acute sense of smell! An early training exercise tells a story.

"We explode into the brilliance above cloud so quickly my eyes ache, hit by the whiteness reflecting the low December sun. I have been above the Scottish clouds before, walking and climbing among the winter hills. But when climbing you surface slowly, step by laboured step, out of the grey mist into the sunlit uplands above. At our Chipmunk's climbing speed of 70 knots the sudden transition from grey cotton-wool stratus to snowy cloud-fields is painful. I have no sun visor to snap shut on the glare. Protective equipment in 1960 is a cloth flying helmet and 'Biggles' flying goggles, not much protection against glare.

The day had started as 'Black Flag' - no flying - with North Sea 'crud' blanketing the Sidlaw Hills and covering Perth Airfield. We are the weather check. We left a soggy grass runway in a visibility of 1000 yards, entered a solid sheet of stratus at 200 feet and are now on top at 3000 feet. We are somewhat delayed. It is late morning but there are a lot of keen new students in the crew room desperate to fly, so we are the first to go.

'Straight and Level Part 2' is the exercise, my fifth flight in a Chipmunk with Glasgow University Air Squadron. My instructor is new on the squadron. He is in the back seat. I am his first pupil; he is my first instructor. We have a lot to teach each other. He is a big man: big in size, big in personality. His previous office in the right hand seat of a Handley Page Victor Mk 1 V-bomber had a bit more space than the back seat of a Chipmunk. He has a commanding presence, complete with RAF moustache, a loud laugh and an inexhaustible fund of risqué jokes revolving around dodgy aircraft, willing women and stupid pilots. He is the incorrigible optimist. We are the first - and only - aircraft airborne and we are relying on Perth Homer, a mythical navigation and recovery aid, published in the airfield directory but never tested in anger by any pilot known to us.

Weather conditions 'on top' are ideal for Straight and Level 2 - zero turbulence, perfect horizon. Even I am making progress. "Keep the lookout scan going", say the voice in the back. Left tailplane, left wing tip, nose, right wing tip, right tailplane, up and over the top and back to left tailplane again. "I want to see your eyeballs from the back cockpit" comes the voice from the back. The patter for Straight and Level 2 unfolds : "Pick an aiming point". Not so easy above a cloud billiard table. "Reduce power, keep straight (wings level, ball in the middle)." I learn to change the attitude, raising the nose as the speed reduces, maintaining height, checking the altimeter; re-trimming. Decreasing power, increasing power. So we go on above the cloud. Sun on the right wing tip, sun on the left wing tip, sun behind, sun in front. New to flying, perhaps, but navigating in the hills and woods by the sun and the clock is not a new experience for me. It is time to go home. "Lets see where 'Perth Homer' puts us?"

'Perth Homer' of course doesn't put us anywhere. Perth Approach announces that 'Perth Homer' requires at least 15 minutes notice to give any information. We are to 'standby'. And so we go on, back and forward, 'Lookout-Power-Attitude-Trim-Lookout.' Twenty minutes later and 'Perth Homer' is still not up and running. I am becoming intrigued as to how we are going to get down. From the northern horizon to the south, from east to west, is solid stratus beneath us. True the cloud base at Perth has lifted to 500 feet and the visibility to 1 mile. But there are high hills around Perth. "Where do you think we are then, Jamieson" comes the voice in the back. "Somewhere around Blairgowrie", I guess. A small town 10 miles north-east of Perth and just south of the high hills of the main Grampian Mountains. "I reckon we are over Dundee" says the voice in the back, a position some 20 miles east of Perth, close to the coast. With the benefit of hindsight I now know that the safety altitude around Dundee is $2500 + 10\% + 1500$ ft $= 4250$ ft and at Blairgowrie is another 1500 feet on top of that. In Lesson 5 of course I do not know that. Ignorance is bliss at this stage of training.

I am sure my instructor knows what he's doing and I trust my instructor. He is the only instructor I have at that moment. He might be beginning to lose his optimism but doesn't show it. For people like him serendipity comes in many forms. In this case it comes as a tiny gap in the cloud-field below. It starts as a tiny gap and through some quirk of vortex or rotor-streaming turbulence around mountains it expands to a small gap.

Down at the bottom of this hole we see a river, a large brown river in a steep-sided valley surrounded by moorland and forest on either side. Around the edge of this gap wisps of cloud trail, unable to make up their mind whether to reform and close the hole or to evaporate altogether. My instructor decides speed is of the essence, tips the Chipmunk on its wing, lowers the nose, pulls to the buffet and we spiral down in a maximum-rate descending spiral with a radius about a Chipmunk's wingspan.

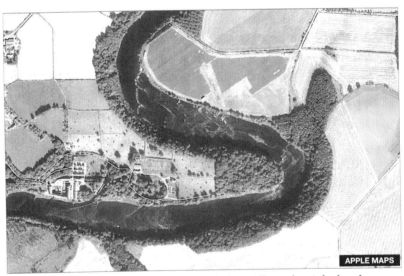

.......double-bend in the river and the mill on the right bank....

We pop out the bottom before the gap closes again and find ourselves in a river valley with grey hills disappearing back up into the cloud on either side. "Perth Homer, Perth

Homer - Steer, Steer" but to no avail. 'Perth Homer' is still not working. The white water of the river rapids point us downstream and we scud along below the cloud-base.

On the nose, the double-bend in the river and the mill on the right bank, give us a fix at the village of Stanley on the River Tay, a few miles north of Perth city – not too far from Blairgowrie. We follow the river down to Perth at 70 knots, half flap in 'poor visibility configuration'. Turn left, past Scone Palace and Old Scone. Keep left of New Scone village and we are lined up on short final approach to the same soggy easterly grass strip that launched us many adventures ago. No one else is airborne!"

Our debrief is short. My instructor has a chat with the Chief Flying Instructor, or vice-versa, about operating from small Scottish airfields in Scottish winter weather.

I learned a bit about 'Straight and Level 2' and "learned a lot about flying from that".

MIGRATION

Once in the sea, the young salmon sets off on its great migrations around the North Atlantic which, after one or more years, bring it back - 'homing' - with great accuracy, to the river of its birth.

The aviator, freshly qualified, sets off on a series of flights, postings and detachments which can take him to strange and distant places from which he must also find his way home again.

6. NAVIGATION FOR SALMON

The Atlantic salmon is famous for its ability to find its way home again to spawn. After years wandering the northern Atlantic for food it finds its way back to the river, even to the gravel bed, where it hatched out from the egg so long ago. Terence Horsley describes the migration graphically in his book *The Long Flight* published in 1947. How does it do that? There are many theories which raise more questions than they answer - and much is still a mystery.

Does it navigate by the sun and the stars? This is long-suspected in other animals and birds - but salmon live under water. Much of the time salmon are believed swim in the upper layers of the sea but they do descend to feed at depth. They might not have a clear sight of celestial guidance at any depth or if the surface of the ocean is agitated by wind or wave? Do they have to leap to take a star shot? How do they do that?

Does it have a built-in magnetic compass? Again, this is suspected in other animals and birds. If so, the salmon and all these species would need to adjust their compass during their travels across the North Atlantic and re-calibrate for changing variation every few years. The angle of 'variation' - the angle between Magnetic North and True North - varies over space and over time. In Scotland in 2020 it was less than 1 degree (West) and changing by 10.5 minutes of a degree (East) each year. But they may be able to compensate for that. How do they do that?

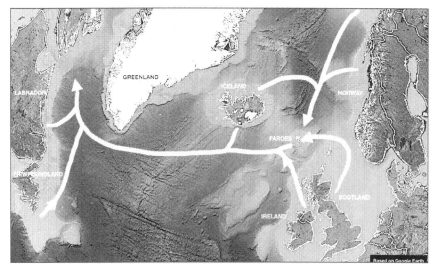

Some salmon migration routes in the North Atlantic

Does it have a built-in Inertial Navigational System (INS)? This would record every acceleration and hence every change of direction, speed and time on the way out - and play it in reverse to find the way back to where it was born. Perhaps the salmon is born with a inbuilt 'memory stick' containing its Flight Plan, or Swim Plan, for its marine migrations. The genetic differentiation of salmon populations within a river system is well-established. But how does one genetic variation know to go to one tributary to spawn and not to the other? Perhaps this is recorded in small variations in their individual Swim Plans in their ancestral DNA. How do they do that?

If these ideas are too fanciful. perhaps it is something simpler. Does the young salmon just hitch a ride on some convenient ocean current, like a 'conveyor belt', heading to the Faroe Islands and then jump currents on to the next one heading for Greenland? It could hitch its way all round the North Atlantic gyre before finding the current to take it back home to where it was born. How do they do that?

Salmon have an exceptionally keen sense of smell and there is evidence that smell has a role to play, at least, in the later stages of homing. An early experiment in North America, demonstrated that Pacific salmon with their noses blocked had only a random chance of finding their natal stream, while the control group with full faculties were much more successful. But does it smell its way all the way home? One would imagine that the North Atlantic has traces of freshwater in microscopic quantities from the Tropics to the Arctic. Whether any specific river could be identified at that range is questionable. How do they do that?

When the salmon does get close to its natal river, how does it cope with dilution and pollution. A salmon looking for the smell of its birthplace at the headwaters of the River Forth system, for example, would have a problem. The chemicals in the River Larig, beyond Balquhidder, which would give it its chemical 'imprint' would be diluted through the lochs of Doine, Voil and Lubnaig before it reached Callander. Further waters from lochs Venachar, Achray and Katrine would increase dilution down to Stirling. Below Stirling, for many generations of salmon, the Forth Estuary was seriously polluted by human and industrial chemicals from Stirling, Alloa, Grangemouth, Rosyth, Edinburgh and Fife. What chance of picking up fragrances of granite, peat and heather from its birthplace in the Larig? How do they do that?

This brings us to the problem of the 'smelly hands'. Your hands - not their's! Given that salmon can smell an angler's prawn or worm (in the old days, remember?) from some distance downstream, how do they cope with an angler's smelly hands? How many Hairy Marys or Waddingtons have been tied on with tobacco-infused fingers. Do salmon prefer pipe tobacco or cigarettes - or nowadays, e-cigarettes? Which aftershave is this season's favourite - or toilet soap? This may not be so fanciful. There is a theory that salmon, especially male salmon, may be susceptible to human female sexual pheromones. That is why women are more successful salmon anglers than men - aren't they? Anyway, I am sure Miss Georgina Ballantine won't give that theory any credit - but that sure was some big male salmon - the 64 lb British record - she caught on the Glendelvine beat of the Tay in 1922.

Perhaps we need to research a bit more whether Willie's greater success at catching salmon is down to his well-crafted skill - or to his aftershave or his morning hand-wash?

7. NAVIGATION FOR SALMON PILOTS

Salmon rivers mean one thing to the angler and another thing to the airman. To the angler the salmon river echoes with the sights and sounds of the countryside, the running water and the occasional fish. To the airmen they can mean life or death. Rivers, big rivers, especially big salmon rivers can mean he is lost among high mountains, covered in cloud, or he is safe in familiar territory using the direction, size, shape and appearance of the river to help him stay on track or on time as he map-reads his way across the landscape. They are also a source of useful information - as I found on an early flight.

"It was 'The Boss' who wanted to fly to Kinloss. He needed an excuse. I was the excuse - a senior student who needs a 'navex' - a navigation exercise. He had friends at Kinloss. There was to be a 'dining-in night'. He would need someone to fly him home the next day. We would take the scenic route, longer, but avoiding the high hills of the Grampians and the Cairngorms where the weather was unpredictable and the cloud was low. We would go from Perth to Kinloss via Aberdeen. I prepared my map with all the approved headings and elapsed times and we set off in a north-easterly direction for Aberdeen. All good so far but soon the map was ignored and I was navigating by salmon rivers."

Rivers of all kinds are very useful for navigation. If they flow close to, or parallel to, track they can be followed, always keeping them on the left-hand side of the aircraft - 'Rules of the Air' - of course. If they converge with your track they can be useful 'funnel' features which can lead to an easily-identified town, bridge or rail junction to confirm your position. If they cross your track they can be useful time-checks and you can plot your 'time-travelled' from river to river. Of course each salmon river also has its own story.

"Setting off from Scone our first time-check was on the River South Esk. This was Terence Horsley's 'Little River'', lovingly described in *Fishing and Flying*. When Horsley flew from Arbroath during the Second World War, he used to extend his landing approach by a few miles so he could see the height of the river at Finavon to check the prospects for fishing later in the evening for salmon and sea trout.

The North Esk is just a little further on beyond the South Esk. Horsley also fished here - night fishing for sea trout just above the tidal pools, where the railway viaduct straddles the river. Already the cloud is descending over the high ground of the Grampians. Out to the left, the Cairn o' Mounth road from Fettercairn to Banchory is dissolving in the mist. Edzell disused airfield is on the left. The longer 'scenic' route, following the coast, was a good decision.

The high ground projects out towards Stonehaven but we can squeeze around it. We call Dyce airfield, cross the famous River Dee, on time, just west of Aberdeen, and turn onto a north-westerly heading for Kinloss.

The River Don is underneath us now as we pass over Kintore and Inverurie. At Inverurie the public salmon fishings were conferred by Robert the Bruce and formally included in a charter by Mary, Queen of Scots, in 1558. The fishings comprise approximately 2 miles on the north bank of the River Don, and approximately a further 2 miles on the west bank of the River Ury. The majority of the Don beats lie upstream of the town. It is a lovely stretch of water passing through wooded countryside, offering splendid views to the Don-side hills. This stretch consists of over a dozen named pools, and its turbulent runs and long glides provide excellent fly water for the salmon angler.

Pilot's view - the River Don at Kintore

The public salmon fishings at Kintore date from the 12th Century and Royal Burgh status was confirmed by James IV in 1506. The River Don here flows for about 2.5 miles through the flood plain giving a range of conditions from streamy to gentle gliding water. The river is significantly bigger in volume after its confluence with the River Ury. The sandy or gravel bottom allows the coverage of most of the 20 named pools, which provide holding lies and a wide variety of water types. Salmon fishing on the Don opens on 11 February and closes on 31 October and both spring and autumn can be prime times. Aberdeenshire Council manage the public fishings at both Inverurie and Kintore.

After the Dee and the Don, the Deveron is the next famous salmon river we cross on our our track to Kinloss. Huntly Town Fishings were gifted to the people of Huntly by the Duke of Gordon and are managed by a committee of local anglers - the Huntly Angling Association - on behalf of the trustees. Visitor permits are available, on the day they are required. Not only are there 38 pools on the Deveron itself but 27 pools on the tributary Bogie and a substantial part of the River Isla.

It is not far from the Deveron to RAF Kinloss. Tuned into the Kinloss Air Traffic Control we can already hear the chatter from the huge Avro Shackleton maritime patrol aircraft, arriving and departing on their 14-hour sorties. We cross the mighty River Spey near Ballindalloch, skirt round to the south of Royal Naval Air Station Lossiemouth - HMS Fulmar - with its new Blackburn Buccaneers. Up ahead is Kinloss. Permission is given to join the circuit and we just have time to take a look at the River Findhorn, to the west of the airfield, before we touch down after our 'scenic' route - navigating by salmon rivers."

Next day, with good weather, we again, navigate back to Perth using salmon rivers, this time as 'line features'. After take-off, it is a quick jump over Dava Moor, and we intercept the Spey at Grantown to see the runs and pools of the Strathspey Angling Association water. Turn right, follow the river south past Aviemore, Loch Insh, Newtonmore and Dalwhinnie and squeeze through the narrow pass at Dalnaspidal. With a good cloud-base we clear the highest point of the route in good order and descend southwards into the Tay system. We pass the dehydrated River Garry, cross Loch Faskally and the Pitlochry salmon ladder and head down the Tummel. The upper River Tay comes in from the right, running down from Loch Tay and Aberfeldy. We are comforted to see a few more fields down here in Strathtay - potential landing grounds if our single engine plays up. Past Dalguise we negotiate the narrow valley around Dunkeld and Birnam - and we are clear of the mountains.

The famous beats of the lower Tay lie to our left - Islamouth, Stobhall, Cargill, Scone, Benchil, Redgorton - and we are cruising across rolling farmland towards the 'Fair City' of Perth. Robert II granted salmon fishing on the Tay to the City of Perth in 1375 and, centuries later, the anglers of the Fair City get the first crack, for a few pounds each year, at mighty salmon which, just a few miles up river would command a thousand pounds a week for the fishing. All the salmon heading for the prestige beats upriver have to negotiate the Perth Town Water and some 300 to 400 salmon are taken each season.

A quick call on the radio alerts Perth Air Traffic Control and we are back on the ground in good order - thanks to Scotland's salmon rivers.

8. SLAVES OF THE WEATHER

Fishers and flyers alike are both slaves of the weather. For our sport or our profession we need to be constantly aware of the vagaries of our volatile atmosphere. "Free as the air." may be a simple platitude to describe the magic of flight or the joy of fishing - but 'air' has a temperature, a pressure, a humidity, a stability. The variation of these attributes produce ice, snow, sun, droughts, rain, floods, wind and gales - all of which have an impact on fishing and flying.

For the flyer, the daily Meteorological Briefing starts early, as early as possible. First he, or she, needs to analyse the 'synoptic chart' - to note the distribution of high pressure areas and low pressure cells, to see the direction and tightness of the isobars between them. From this they may identify the warm fronts, the cold fronts and the occluded fronts which will bring different patterns of rain, wind and visibilities.

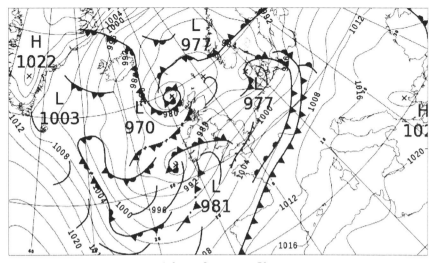
A busy Synoptic Chart

For the fisher, the same chart may indicate where and when the heaviest rain may fall and how far in advance of their fishing trip. It should tell them how cold it might be or how windy. There is even a school of thought that fish can be affected by atmospheric pressure. Logically, they should be. The surface of the water feels the same pressure as the surface of the land. Fish feel aquatic pressures through the sensors on their 'lateral line' - so should be able to feel increasing or decreasing atmospheric pressures. There are many theories as to how the changing atmospheric pressure might affect fish taking-behaviour. Are fish more active when the pressure is high? Are fish unsettled when the pressure is low? Do fish take better when the pressure is rising - or falling? We may have our own experiences and theories.

For the flyer the details of the weather make the difference of a successful trip or an aborted sortie. Getting down to the details, the flyer needs to know, not just the wind at ground-level, but all the way up to the altitude he will be flying. He needs to know what the cloud structure will be as height increases. He needs to know the weather, not just en-route, but at his destination, some miles away and hours later.

Pilot's view - Trouble ahead

Some specific numbers are significant. When flying below 3000 feet, if the visibility reduces to less than 5 km during flight he can no longer continue under Visual Flight Rules, keeping his own lookout. If he is flying between 3000 and 10,000 feet he must have 1500 metres horizontal clearance and 1000 feet vertical clearance from cloud. If the weather does not allow this then the pilot has to continue under Instrument Flight Rules, which are more complicated and require a Flight Plan. At his destination, if the cloud base is below a certain height above the runway, or if the visibility is below a minimum - he may not land.

So the details of the weather are important for the flyer. And we can always get caught out!

"I had to fly from Glasgow to Dyce for an important event. The Boss had politely asked if I was going up the previous day to stay overnight and make sure we all got there in good order. But the weather forecast was good and I wanted another night at home with my family. So I confirmed I would fly up to Dyce on the next day.

Come the day, the weather forecast was still good - cloud and visibility OK at the 3000-4000 feet we would transit. We set off out by Dumbarton in the clear, turned right at Balloch and started to climb. The sky was clear blue alright but the whole route below us, towards Aberdeen was covered in fog - ground-hugging fog. Not even the 2000 ft hills - the Ochils and Southern Highlands were clear to mark the edges of Strathallan and Strathearn. So we had no options for a forced landing if our single-engine played up but we could always bale-out from 3000 ft!

Intending to map-read, I had made only a sketchy flight plan and our only navigation aid was our VHF radio with ten preset channels, two of which were 'common' frequencies and should be 'listened out' by most stations. Seeking some reassurance I called Perth. No answer. I called Dyce. No answer. I could still hear some chatter from Glasgow far behind me but that was not much use. Leuchars was a Master Diversion airfield open 24/7 and should be listening out on common frequencies. I called Leuchars. No answer. Don't like this much, stuck above clouds, no navigation aids and nobody speaking to me. So I swallowed my pride and called the Emergency Frequency - 121.5 MHz. Bliss, back came a response. We were not lost anymore. Scottish Centre at Prestwick alerted Leuchars to listen out on our frequency and they gave us a steer towards their overhead.

En-route to Leuchars a large hole - a "sucker gap" - appeared in the cloud below us and showed me the Tay Road Bridge and the coast of Angus. I said 'thank you' to Leuchars, eased down through the hole and headed up the coast towards Aberdeen at 1000 ft. Alas, the cloud base came lower. Soon we were flying just off the coast at 500 ft, not a clever thing to do in a single-engined aircraft, below bale-out height and with no dinghy or sea-survival kit. Even less clever when we neared the Fowlsheugh seabird colonies and watched 10 lb seagulls and gannets whizz past the wingtips and over the canopy hoping that they would not

get chopped up in the propeller or get stuffed in the cooling air intake in the front of the Gypsy Major engine. We made it - and crept sheepishly across the coast at Aberdeen and with some relief plonked onto the runway at Dyce.
"I learned about flying from that...

The fisher has more tolerance of the weather but it is still important. Yes, on a river he may get wet or stay dry. He may have an upstream or a downstream wind. He may get cold or warm. There may be glaring sunshine or useful cloud cover. If he examines the synoptic chart he may anticipate where the rain is going to fall in the watershed, work out when the rise in water will reach his beat and plan accordingly. He might work out that a night's hard frost in the uplands is going to drop his river level until it thaws again. How is the snow in the mountains going to melt? Is it going to melt suddenly under a downpour of a warm front from an Atlantic low to produce a dirty flood or will it melt slowly in the warming sun of a ridge of high pressure just to keep the water at a nice height for fishing. It is all useful to know about the weather.

There is much evidence that Scotland's weather is become more extreme as a result of the changing climate. This affects flyers and fishers. Flyers are encountering more frequent storm events, stronger winds, heavier and more prolonged rainfalls. Fishers are finding more volatile rivers - rising and falling more frequently and rapidly with extreme droughts and low water or heavy floods. It pays to know these things!

9. DESIGNED TO TRAVEL

It should come as no surprise that the aeroplane is designed to look like a salmon - or vice-versa. They both have to manoeuvre and survive in a fluid in motion - either air or water. They do not share all the forces in the same way but there are enough similarities. The main difference is that water is much denser than air and the forces are stronger at lower current or air speeds.

Evolution has carefully shaped the salmon to minimize its resistance to the water around it, enabling it to travel vast distances with ease and to display, when necessary, to our great delight, sudden bursts of speed. We note that if Mother Nature decided that a proper fish would require a girth to accommodate muscles, gut, swim-bladder, and reproductive organs, then she would design a fish with the cross-section of an average salmon. If she now wanted it to travel thousands of miles across oceans, out-run predators, run long distances against all odds up-river and provide heart-stopping bursts of speed for fortunate fishermen, she would design it for minimum resistance to the water - minimum drag.

A 20-ton Canberra

A 20-pound salmon

Physiologically, the most rapid swimming-speed which fish can indefinitely sustain is around 1 body-length-per-second. For a grilse of around 60cm, 1 body-length-per-second equates to around 50 km per day. Tagging experiments have demonstrated how far and how fast some Scottish salmon can travel. One fish, tagged on the west coast of Scotland was recaptured in the Firth of Forth - 9 days and 490 km later. This fish had moved at an average speed of around 55 km per day. So, this long-distance traveller must have been swimming near its maximum sustainable rate between Loch Inchard and the Forth.

The forces affecting an aircraft wing in flight are - Lift, opposing Weight, to get it off the ground and Drag, opposing the Thrust which wants to move it forward. Lift is generated by the fluid (air) moving across a curved or cambered surface (a wing). Drag is created by the motion of the same fluid (air) past the same surface. A salmon does not need to worry about weight and can adjust its weight to zero by its internal swim bladder. In a salmon, thrust is generated by the lateral movement of its tail. By flexing its body into a cambered shape the salmon can create a force, similar to lift, in all three dimensions - up, down and sideways.

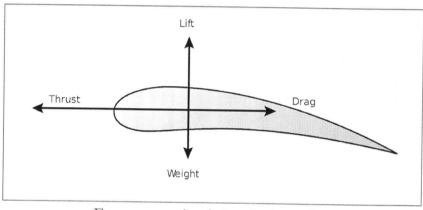

Forces on a cambered aircraft wing in flight

Drag comes from three main sources. First, from the shape of the fish, so-called 'profile drag', second, from the properties of its skin, a source of drag known as 'skin friction' and thirdly from what is known as 'interference drag' caused by essential design features like fins interfering with the streamlined shape.

1. *Profile Drag:* If, by way of experiment, you should stick your hand into the water, at right angles to the river flow, you would receive an impression of the maximum amount of drag on that particular cross-sectional shape, at that water speed. The smooth water flow separates behind the plate creating turbulence, suction and hence, maximum drag. To maintain smooth water flow around the salmon for as long as possible and reduce drag to a minimum, we need the familiar streamlined shape of an aerofoil. Not by coincidence, that is the shape of a salmon. The profile drag is now only a small percentage of the original value for a flat hand of the same cross-sectional area

and all muscle, gut, swim bladder and reproductive organs are neatly incorporated into the design. Such are the wonders of nature.

2. *Skin Friction:* But the wonders do not stop there for the salmon is even more cleverly designed. Some drag takes the form of skin friction produced in the very thin (less than one millimetre) layer of water close to the skin of the fish. This is called the 'boundary layer'. You will have to accept the fact that, despite the relative speed between the salmon and the current, the actual molecules of water that are in contact with the skin are, in fact, static. The logic of this is undeniable otherwise the salmon's coat of slime would be continually washed away. However, all the other layers of water which make up this boundary layer slide upon each other like a pack of cards, each one sliding faster the further away it is from the skin itself until the outer edge of the boundary layer is travelling at the same speed as the flow of the stream.

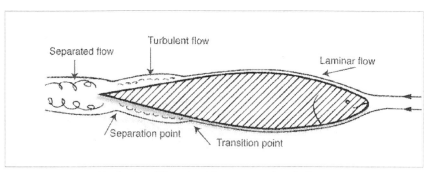

Reducing 'Drag' with a streamlined shape

The secret of minimum drag is to keep the flow smooth and attached to the skin - a 'laminar flow' - in the boundary layer. This is helped by a lovely smooth skin, covered in scales and slime. With the streamlined aerofoil shape, the boundary layer remains laminar with minimum drag, until the 'transition point' when it becomes turbulent, producing a bit more drag. Further back, at the 'separation point', however, the boundary layer becomes detached from the skin and starts to create significantly more drag. The salmon's shape, therefore, delays separation until the last possible moment, and the use of the anal fin and the adipose fin can re-energise the boundary layer towards the tail of the fish to enable the flow to remain attached even longer.

3. *Interference Drag.* Another little design challenge resolved by the salmon in its quest for speed is that of 'interference drag'. Where fins, or anything else, stick out from an otherwise streamlined shape, interference drag is created. This factor is reduced by moulding the fins smoothly into the body with shapes called 'fillets'. Anglers find such fillets as the 'wrist' useful for tailing their salmon but their primary purpose is streamlining. So the salmon is not just designed so that it fits neatly into your salmon bass. Evolution has carefully designed it to minimise the resistance from the water to enable it to travel vast distances and to display that burst of speed to thrill us anglers – if we can hook one.

Built To Fight

The great attraction of the salmon for the angler, of course, is its fighting quality, its ability to thrill with speed, vigour, and power in the swirling currents of its native element, testing tackle and angler to the limit. Like all fish, the salmon has a number of ways of manoeuvring in its watery environment. In any still or running water it can adjust its depth, up or down, in the water column by altering the amount of gas in its swim bladder, thereby altering its apparent buoyancy in the water. This involves no dynamic forces at all and allows the grey shape in the pool to sink out of sight of the angler without disturbance to the water. Another common way for the fish to manoeuvre is to point itself in the direction it wants to go, vigorously flap its tail and rear body, and swim there. This is the simplest trick that the salmon uses in its headlong dash down the pool when it first feels the tension of the line.

The cunning design of the salmon comes into its own when the fish works its way into fast currents and can apply the aerodynamic shape to generate its own special forces. Even when not inclined at an angle to the current, the cambered shape generates forces as a result of the acceleration of the stream flow around the curvatures varying the resultant pressure distribution. The magnitude of these pressure changes can be influenced by the angle to the current and the curvature, or 'camber', of the shape itself. Because a salmon is rounded in cross-section, it can generate forces in both the vertical plane and in the horizontal plane.

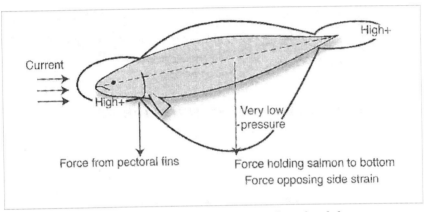

Pressure distribution on a salmon with its head down

These pressure changes generate a lot more force than would be expected from the fish itself. The use of these forces can give the salmon, in flowing water, a strength and energy apparently out of all proportion to its size and weight. This ability can cause the angler a few hairy moments. Can the fish be subdued? Or, if it breaks the tackle it must have been huge? The effect of all this science on the salmon, fighting at the end of your line, is twofold. First, by getting its head down in the current it can generate a strong enough downforce to keep it on the bottom of the river. When the assistance of its massive pectoral fins is added, it is no wonder that such a fish takes some shifting from the stones at the bottom of the white water. A second effect is that, by curving its spine sideways and increasing its effective camber, the salmon can generate a massive lateral force to oppose your side-strain. This requires relatively little exertion from the fish, apart from retaining its curved shape. It is then a question of patience and muscle power as to whether you or the salmon tires first.

So the salmon is not just a pretty shape. It has a few secret weapons up its scales when it comes to confrontation with an angler. So don't feel too despondent when the next one gets away. Just think of all those lifts and drags and velocities and wonder how you managed to hook the beast in the first place.

10. RHINELAND

In the 1960s I found myself in Germany flying Canberra bombers from the west bank of the River Rhine. The Rhine was a big part of our life in Germany. Most days we flew across it on our way to exercises. It appeared as a dirty, muddy, industrial river full of barges carrying coal and other industrial goods between Rotterdam and the Ruhr. The Rhine did not come to mind as a salmon river. Yet the Rhine was once the largest salmon-producing river in Europe. A hundred years ago, a million salmon were migrating between Greenland, the Rhine and its tributaries all the way up as far as the Swiss Alps. But the original strain of these Rhine fish had suffered great loss over the years. By the 1950s, salmon had gradually disappeared from the Rhine river basin.

We were based in Germany as part of NATO's 2ATAF (Second Allied Tactical Air Force) providing a nuclear deterrent force against the Warsaw Pact across the Iron Curtain in Eastern Europe. In the 1950s a group of four new airfields known as 'The Clutch' had been constructed on the sandy terrace to the west of the Rhine - Geilenkirchen, Wildenrath, Bruggen and Laarbruch.

Initially the Canberra had seemed a heavy and docile aircraft compared to the tiny Folland Gnat but we were now flying the B(I)8 (Bomber/Interdictor Mk 8) version which proved a very powerful and nimble beast. The B(I)8 was newer and heavier than the old B2, with more powerful Avon Mk 109 engines. It had a 'fighter-type' cockpit, offset above the fuselage, and offering a 360 degree view above and around the aircraft. It carried more fuel, so had longer legs. Much of the time it was a steady mount but on a low-level bombing run-in to target at Nordhorn or Tarhuna ranges we flew at 434 knots at 250 feet. At that speed the controls were very heavy and the wide wings responded to every gust of turbulence. It needed serious muscle power to make any control adjustments at that speed. This was particularly so in the early days when we were performing the Low Altitude Bombing System (LABS) manoeuvre. This involved pulling up into a half-loop to lob the bomb onto the target followed by a roll-off the top at 5000 feet and a steep dive in the opposite direction to escape the blast (hopefully). The music from Wagner's *Ride of the Valkyries* was always somewhere in the background and it is difficult to match that level of adrenaline in anything else - except salmon fishing. "They whom the Gods would destroy....... they allow to do LABS in a Canberra" . At a later date we converted to a Lay-Down delivery. Not quite so physically challenging but an equal adrenaline rush at 600 feet on a dark night!

My navigator, John was a young Pilot Officer - quiet, watchful, reserved - but with a dry sense of humour. He had grown up in my part of Scotland and spoke the same language. We crewed-up at Bassingbourn, understood each other, just stayed that way and had been posted to Germany together. Flying with John, we achieved our coveted 'combat' status and provided a deterrent to the 'Evil Empire' behind the Iron Curtain. Our 3 years and 600 flying hours together were a kaleidoscopic adventure and included many of the 'firsts' we experienced as a rookie Canberra crew:

• Long low-level cross-country flights around North Germany, in sunshine and thunderstorms;

• Crossing the Alps at 45000 feet, far above any airliners and where the sky is almost black;

• Finding the brown dot of Malta somewhere in the murky 'goldfish bowl' of the Mediterranean on our first Southern Ranger.

• Crawling out of our bunks at 4 am in Malta to take-off in darkness to get to Idris Field, Tripoli, and get some low level bombing in before the turbulence made life impossible.

• Landing and taking off on Gibraltar's tiny runway and upsetting the Spanish authorities.

Low Level

"We accelerate down the runway ahead of 15,000 lbs of thrust from two Rolls Royce Avon 109 engines. We unstick at 140 knots and climb to 1000 feet, turning east. From his navigator's position, prone in the nose of the Canberra, John map-reads the anatomy of the North German Plain. Hills and valleys are the bones of the country. Fields, woods and forest flesh it out. Roads and railways carry its lifeblood. Towns and villages are the nerve centres. The River Rhine, looms up ahead - the large bowel of Western Europe - sending its urban and industrial wastes to the North Sea. We cross the Rhine at right angles at Xanten. East of the Rhine we drop down to our low-flying altitude of 250 feet. The world speeds up. Red roofs, tree tops, road signs - flash past beneath us. Twenty minutes into mission we approach the Teutoburgerwald, the Osnabruch Ridge, that long finger of hills and masts jutting northwards into the North German Plain, the last high ground before the Ural Mountains in Russia.

Canberra B(I)8 at low level

We fly east towards the Iron Curtain between East and West Germany, separating the Free World from the Soviets. We penetrate beneath the Buffer Zone and head towards the Air Defence Identification Zone (ADIZ). We visualise, across the border, perhaps, a pair of East German MIG 21 fighters scrambling to intercept us as potential intruders, wasting scarce fuel and aircraft hours and testing the patience of the pilots. We never know. We turn left, heading north, parallel the ADIZ, following the River Elbe. With Hamburg on the nose we swing left again, heading west, pick up the Kusten Kanal and head for our bombing range at Nordhorn with our practice bomb for our First Run Attack (FRA). Nordhorn Range Controller comes on the radio. We are cleared to run in. John guides us on to a final attack heading. We accelerate to 434 knots and I struggle to hold the twenty-ton bomber down at 250 feet against the nose-up trim. Thirty seconds to target. Bomb switches - ON - and the adrenalin increases. Five seconds to run. 'Bomb gone'. I pull up, decelerating. Bomb switches – OFF. Call - 'Clear Range'. We head back to base. Range Safety radios our result in the 'Code of the Day'. A ten-yard undershoot. Not bad when our real bomb has a rather larger radius of total destruction.

We return to base. At 1000 feet we enter cloud and climb to 3000 feet. The warm front from the North Sea has come in early. Cloud and fog at base are 'on the deck'. The radar operator picks us up, well out from the field and the reassuring voice of the WRAF controller, starts talk-down. "You are right of the centreline. Turn left five degrees, 265. You are on the centreline, turn right three degrees, 268. You are approaching the glide-path, prepare to lose height. Surface wind 250/15 knots," soothes the voice. The aircraft flies itself, the needles never flicker. "You are on the centreline, on the glide-path.," the voice reassures. "You are cleared to land from this approach. Reaching radar touchdown - now. I can offer no further service. Change to Tower frequency on Stud 1 now." With a slight squeal the big rubber tyres contact the runway, slow down with a touch of the toe brakes and rumble gently to the end of the runway."

High Level

Just as the salmon follows its imprinted migration routes around the North Atlantic so we aviators had our Standard Routes around the sky to achieve our end-game. We had many high-level flights. Our worst one was a three-and-a-half hour night sortie up to Norway, over to Stornoway, down to Wales and back to Germany. This was used by the squadron to catch up on night-flying hours to make the monthly target. Three-and-a-half hours of exquisite freezing boredom only broken by heading changes and oxygen checks.

"It is quiet in the cockpit. The steady hum of the twin Rolls Royce Avon engines provides a calming background. The occasional rumble from a compressor reminds me of their age. The cockpit is suffused in a warm orange glow from the cockpit lighting, turned low to avoid distractions and reflections. The cockpit feels a safe cocoon of civilisation up in this hostile night-time environment, 40,000 feet above the winter North Sea. But it is cold. The outside air temperature at cruising height is always around minus 56 degrees Centigrade - summer and winter. Inside the cockpit it is not much warmer and we don't yet have 'bunny suits' and immersion suits or electric socks. The Canberra heating is legendary and bad. The cabin pressurisation is equally basic - usually estimated at half the outside pressure, plus 2000 ft. So at 40,000 ft (or Flight Level 400 - to us pilots) the pressure inside the cabin is around 22,000 feet - not very healthy for long periods and conducive to the 'bends'. We are also breathing 100% oxygen under pressure. This ends up in body tissues and, when sleeping, can expand into the inner ears, with painful and sometimes catastrophic results for eardrums."

In our wanderings in the oceans of the air we had our own favoured migration routes where we could mix with our own cohorts and share the wisdom and knowledge of air travel. Our favourite high-level flights were crossing the Alps at 45000 feet, down to Malta. RAF Luqa on Malta, was always a popular destination. The island was still very pro-British with a post-colonial flavour about it. It was the crossroads, or Piccadilly Circus, of the RAF. The Transit Mess was always full of scruffy aircrew in flying kit, night-stopping en-route to Cyprus, Persian Gulf, Aden, Gan or Singapore. We were down every six weeks to start with, practicing bombing on the range at Tarhuna in Libya. We knew many of the aircrew transitting through Malta. Paddy brought his Beverley down, heading for Khormakhsar, Aden. Dave was already based at RAF Hal Far on his Shackletons. Ian was an Operations Officer at Luqa. Single-engined Hunters staged through on their way to Aden. Four-engined Hastings transports ferried kit around the Mediterranean and the Middle East. Delta-winged Vulcan bombers of the V-Force staged through on their way to Singapore and Malaysia, via Gan, to show the flag. There were Canberras everywhere. The four Germany strike squadrons rotated down for training with much rivalry and bad behaviour. There were two resident Canberra Photo-Reconnaissance (PR) squadrons plus the four Germany PR squadrons also ripe for challenge. There were Near East Air Force (NEAF) strike squadrons at Akrotiri in Cyprus who often visited Malta for a change of scene. It was a lively detachment and we invariably knew someone, who knew someone - who knew us!

Was it worth it? Well! - the Berlin Wall was breached in 1989 and demolished in 1991, the same year that the Soviet Union collapsed.

Return of the Rhine Salmon

Anthony Netboy, in his *Atlantic Salmon: A Vanishing Species,* describes some of the earlier glories of the salmon fishery in the Rhine, when they were famous delicacies in the cafes of Paris and Berlin. One deep pool on the river, by the Lorelie, is reputed to have provided local fishermen with 6000 salmon each year. In the 1880s the nets and seines in the Dutch section of the Rhine alone produced millions of pounds of salmon yearly. In 1886, a convention was signed by the German Empire, the Netherlands and the Swiss Confederation to protection the Rhine salmon but was ineffective. Industrial and domestic pollution and hydro-electric dams continued to take their toll. Catches slumped around the First World War and petered out in the 1940s.

In the past 30 years, however, the International Commission for the Protection of the Rhine (ICPR) has improved water quality and the ecological continuity of the river and has partly restored the biodiversity of the Rhine basin. A number of major modifications have been made to the Rhine tributaries to make dams more surmountable for fish, in particular, by the construction of fish passes and ladders. A re-introduction plan for salmon, initiated by the ICPR in 1991, has been very successful. Natural spawning now occurs in the Sieg, the Lahn and the lower part of the Ill, in Alsace. In the Mosel, a lot of dams have been removed to allow fish migration and natural re-colonization. Salmon can once again return to the Kinzig, in Baden-Wurtemberg, a river once teeming with fish. The majority of its course, with its all-important spawning areas, is now accessible with re-colonisation supported by hatchery introductions. Since fish ladders were added to the Iffezheim and Gambsheim hydroelectric dams, salmon have been able to swim upstream again all the way to Strasbourg, but their journey ends there.

Four more French dams (Gerstheim, Rhinau, Marckolsheim and Vogelgrün) block their migratory path. If these dams became passable, salmon could once again populate both new Black Forest tributaries and their original spawning beds in Switzerland, as many of the dams in the Black Forest and in Switzerland have already been equipped with fishways. The battle for the salmon is not over. The "Salmon Come Back" campaign was launched by WWF Switzerland and coordinated internationally with other NGO's, federal organizations and private sponsors from different countries.

If the salmon reach Basel, the spawning areas in the Upper Rhine and its tributaries would all be available for reproduction, which would mean a doubling of the spawning and juvenile habitats in one go!

11. IN THE SOUTH

From 5000 feet above Hungerford, the River Kennet and its valley are a dark green thread among the fields, woods and gallops of the Berkshire Downs. From this height I cannot see the limpid chalk stream, the gently waving weed and the ample trout - but I can imagine them. I can visualise Terence Horsley, standing by the side of his own chalk stream, wherever it was, in 1940, sharing an evening's fishing with a new friend after a day's flying, when:

" ... the peace of the evening was suddenly shattered" he writes, "A high whine from the supercharger of a Merlin engine cut through the still air, and, looking up, we saw the graceful shape of a Hurricane casting its silhouette against the sky. …..My companions eyes followed it and .. on his face was a curious, animated, expression as though he was excited. His eyes followed it until it was out of sight, and then he drew a deep unconscious breath as though something disturbing had passed out of his mind....... And then, of course, I knew.... He flew one himself, and when I asked him, he said that his squadron had been pretty busy these last few weeks."

Horsley and his friend arranged to meet on the following Sunday. He never came. Horsley never discovered what became of him - in that summer of 1940.

My travels with an aeroplane take me to other hallowed waters, not always with a fishing rod, but with an admiring mind. Instructor school in the Cotswolds exposed me to the delightful streams of the upper Thames - the Windrush and the Evenlode. I stood in Bourton-on-the-Water and admired the speckled trout camouflaged against the gravel bottom. Visits to Wiltshire gave me an afternoon on a tiny chalk stream near Colerne for which I had to send £5 in arrears to the owner, to salve my conscience, because I had forgotten to pay my fee at the time. Summer Camp at St Mawgan introduced me to my first rainbow trout when an afternoon's fishing on Porth Reservoir, netted a couple of shining trout which were cooked by the Mess kitchen for Squadron breakfast.

Travels with Erich were different and always exciting. Erich first appeared at the bar of the Squadron Mess in Glasgow one evening. I have no idea who let him in or checked his identity. He was tall, thin, long-limbed with the motion of a large uncoordinated puppy. He introduced himself as Erich, with a slightly exaggerated old-fashioned mid-European charm. His hair was long and oiled and his toothbrush moustache was out of kilter for young men in 1960s Glasgow. He might have been an East German spy?

He claimed to be a fellow-student, albeit a mature one, a member of the Officer's Training Corps (OTC) - the Army's equivalent of the Air Squadron at the University. He had always had the ambition to be a pilot, he said, but was rejected on eyesight grounds. As second choice he was now an officer cadet in the OTC intending to join the Regular Army and try for the Special Air Service (SAS).

Erich had adopted the Squadron and managed to cadge some flights as a passenger on air tests and staff continuation training but his other ambition was to join the SAS. To do so he had to pass rigorous, as in 'RIGOROUS', long-distance 'yomps' and survival exercises usually in the Brecon Beacons. So to the Brecon Beacons we had to go. Erich scrounged a Land Rover for the weekend. I don't know where and I did not dare ask but off we went with vehicle, tents and survival rations for the weekend. I took my fishing rod. We camped in the hills somewhere near Brecon. Erich went 'yomping' and I went off to catch some breakfast. It was only sunrise when I found this delightful river, cast my way downstream, caught a couple of trout, one of which was breakfast-sized and eventually returned to base. It was only later, much later, that I discovered I had been a naughty boy. Firstly, I had had no rod-licence (we did not require rod licences in Scotland). Secondly, I had been fishing an exclusive beat on the River Usk, much favoured by the, then, legendary Lionel Sweet and Oliver Kite. Thirdly, I had killed and eaten a trout instead of putting it back to live another day. It was all Erich's fault, of course, and he never did make the SAS.

A tour in Yorkshire gave me a longer opportunity to enjoy fishing in the south. My first introduction to Yorkshire fishing was in Leeming Beck which ran close by the eponymous airfield. This was an eye-opener for me. The beck was deep and clear and full of grayling. You could see the grayling down close to the bottom in the clear water. This was where Frank Sawyer's nymphs and techniques made sense. Up in Scotland, on the Clyde, I had tried Sawyer's Grey Goose and Pheasant Tail nymphs with mixed success, unable to see the grayling but casting in faith to where they ought to be. But here, in the beck, I could see the grayling, could sink the nymph 'just so', see the pale opening of the mouth and strike at just the right time. Not quite fishing in a barrel - but not far away! I also had my first introduction to predatory chub. In a deeper pool further upstream I had hooked a small grayling which was making a splash about coming ashore. As I was about to unhook it, I was aware of a large shadow following behind it in the water - a very large shadow indeed which seemed intent on my grayling. Eventually the shape acquired a pair of large eyes and a large mouth and morphed into the biggest chub I have ever seen - or imagined. Just as quickly it reversed back into the dark pool and I was left with my small grayling which was probably not best pleased to be returned to the same pool as the monster chub. Hey ho! That's conservation.

There was plenty other interesting fishing in North Yorkshire. The River Swale at Richmond and at Morton was very accessible and the River Ure at Tanfield was not. Tanfield was judged to be the 'creme de la creme' in this part of the world but was a private club with no day tickets. The accessible water at Richmond covered several miles and included the Marske Beck. Wednesday afternoons were designated sports afternoons in the RAF in those days and while others were kicking footballs or cracking willow, I headed for the Swale above Richmond. It was a charming river, a free-stone river, running clear and cool off the Millstone Grit and limestone of the northern Pennines. There were plenty pools and runs and lots of fly-life to keep me happy for my two fishing seasons there.

I confess to a slight embarrassment on the Marske Beck one day. After an overnight's rain, the beck was in good ply with a slight colour to a good height of water. It cried out for a wee worm of which I just happened to have a few - as we would in my part of Scotland. In a glorious day's sport I worked my way up the beck plopping a worm into each pool and invariably catching take-able trout up to one pound in weight. After a breakfast basket of half-a dozen, they all went back but it was good sport and a tribute to the fertility and generosity of the little beck. All was good and I was in good spirits until I met the bailiff at the bottom of the beck. "Had I had any luck?' he asked politely. "Yes", I assured him anxious to display my success. "Nice fish", says he, "and what fly were they taking today". "Oh! It was worms today", said I. The bailiff changed colour. "Have you not read your permit?" he asked. I began to feel hot under the colour. What crime had I committed? "No," I confessed. I had not read my permit in detail. "Ah!", said the bailiff stroking his chin sagely. "You will not know that it is 'fly-only' on the beck, then". I think my expression told him that I had been unaware of this rule and that I was mighty embarrassed at having infringed such a holy edict as a visitor to this well-managed and accessible water. The bailiff was reassured and we parted on good terms with a strong recommendation and mental note to read my permit in more detail in the future.

Life was not all fishing in Yorkshire. As part of my role I was expected to be familiar with the Jet Provost but I suspected that the real reason for my posting was to provide a Chipmunk-qualified glider-tug pilot for the Clevelands Gliding Club based at RAF Dishforth some 5 miles down the A1 from Leeming. Many Sundays saw me towing gliders into the air from Dishforth, struggling off to the skies above Ripon, searching for the elusive 'standing waves' coming off the Pennines or just picking up some up-currents from the dales around Ripon. It was a reminder of Terence Horsley again and his classic book *Soaring Flight* and the original standing waves he discovered over the Grampian Mountains all those years ago.

HOMING

After one or more years wandering in the oceans the salmon returns to the river of its birth. On returning to its native river the salmon continues upstream until it eventually reaches the pools and gravels where it was born.

Every flight starts from a base, usually an airfield. After its travels the aircraft returns to refuel and repair for its next flight. The aviator, too, returns to his base to review his route and to file his next Flight Plan.

12. SOARING LOCH LOMOND

We take off from the westerly runway at Glasgow Airport and turn right heading for Dumbarton. Although Glasgow Airport is protected by a Air Traffic Control Zone, where aircraft are obliged to fly under complex Instrument Flight Rules, light aircraft, like our Chipmunk, have dispensation to exit the Control Zone by special Entry/Exit Lanes, under what are called Special Visual Flight Rules (SVFR) where we promise 'to keep clear of cloud and within sight of the surface'. That is no problem today as there are clear skies and unlimited visibility. The student in the front cockpit is doing well - a senior student with lots of experience. I can relax a little bit and enjoy the ride.

At Dumbarton, we turn north following the River Leven up to our Local Flying Area around Loch Lomond. Following the River Leven north, we keep the river on our left-hand side. One of the 'Rules of the Air' - when following a 'line-feature' always keep the feature on the left-hand side of the aircraft. Why? Because there will be bound to be someone else using the same line-feature for navigation and you don't want to hit them head-on. So keeping the River Leven on our left allows incoming aircraft to follow the river inbound to Glasgow Airport on the other side with good separation between us. No problem!

Assured by this safety procedure, I can spare a few moments to look down at the River Leven and wonder at the legions of salmon and sea trout that each year make their way through this industrial valley up to Loch Lomond and into the spawning tributaries of Endrick, Fruin, Luss and Falloch. By the same token I can visualise the legions of anglers, from the Leven valley, Glasgow and industrial Clydeside, who have fished and looked after the river for over 100 years.

"The fishing on the River Leven and Loch Lomond is managed by the Loch Lomond Angling Improvement Association. This august body has its origins in 1860 when a group of eight gentlemen got together to take a one-year lease of the sea trout and salmon net fishings of the River Leven for a sum of £90, "with a view to improving the fishing in Loch Lomond and its tributaries." In 1896 the Association obtained 33 convictions for poaching. In the same year it spent £70 on the purchase of 150,000 trout ova for Loch Lomond and spent another £10 as a contribution to the cost of removing falls on the River Endrick.

In 1890 the Association obtained the services of an enthusiastic secretary, in the shape of Henry Lamond. Lamond's experiences are written-up in his classic book, *Loch Lomond - A Study in Angling Conditions*. He realised that the future of the Association lay in achieving two objectives. Firstly, there was a need for greater public support and recognition of their work and, secondly, they needed wider control over the whole river and estuary system where the migratory fish lived and bred to achieve the integrated management of the salmon and sea trout resource.

Between 1901 and 1930 membership increased from 123 to 610 and the Association controlled the tidal Gareloch and Clyde at Dumbarton and Renfrew, the River Leven, Loch Lomond and the Luss and Fruin tributaries. In 1930 they obtained a lease over 10 miles of the Endrick, the main spawning tributary of the loch, and Lamond's aims had been realised. The Association continues to the present day as one of the most respected angling associations serving the northern half of the Clydeside conurbation."

We clear our exit-lane at Balloch and climb up above Loch Lomond to carry out our exercises. On a clear day we could look down and count the fishing boats on the water and see which part of the loch they were fishing - a useful guide as to whether and where it was worth going later in Campbell's boat. On a very sunny day you could clearly see that magic boundary where the light-coloured shallows shelved into the dark brown of the deeper water - where the salmon usually lay.

"Ian Wood knew where Loch Lomond salmon lay. Ian was an early editor of *Trout and Salmon* magazine and had some amazing catches on the loch. He relates some of his tales in his book *My Way with Salmon,* published in 1957. One day he boated 7 salmon weighing 77.5 lb. On another occasion he had 5 salmon for 67 lb. One day of 3 salmon included a 32.5 lb fish. Even on the tributary River Endrick he could charm the Loch Lomond salmon catching 5 salmon for 55 lb in under 1.5 hours! By 1957 Ian had landed over 1000 salmon.

Ian only ever used one pattern of fly, a gold body with a black and white turkey wing, in various sizes when he fished for salmon in lochs. His theory was that having confidence in the fly and the way it is fished is more important than the pattern of fly. "If you are not happy with your fly, you fish with doubt in your mind. Your mental state lacks that calm, purposeful, determined outlook that the fisher must have." His theory seemed to work, at least for him. Ian's knowledge of Loch Lomond was encyclopaedic, particularly where the salmon would be lying in all the different conditions of wind, weather and water levels and his ability to manoeuvre the boat over the likely lies where the shallows gave way to deeper water created success. In loch fishing for salmon, says Ian, ".....the most important thing to watch is the depth; and if you are in any doubt always err on the shallow side. Most of my loch salmon have been taken in water between 3 and 6 feet deep......"

I fished Loch Lomond occasionally during my time at Glasgow. Campbell, one of my student pilots, had a beautifully-maintained, clinker-built 16-foot Orkney open boat, moored at Balloch. At various times over my three-year tour, he would take us, more on an 'adventure', than a fishing trip, around the loch. True, we would cast a fly on a few drifts and learned a bit from watching other anglers. I tried to get Campbell to follow Ian Wood's advice and follow the shoreline just where the sandy shallows edged down into the darker depths around the islands but I never did hook one of Ian Wood's monsters.

Soaring

On the east side of Loch Lomond are two curiously-shaped hills - Conic Hill and Gualann - which forms part of the Highland Boundary Fault between the hard rocks of the Highlands and the softer sandstones of the Lowlands. They form a barrier and, in particular winds from the west, a peculiar updraft occurs. In certain conditions of atmospheric stability this updraft can lead to the formation of a 'standing wave', which oscillates downwind at high level - a phenomenon desired by glider pilots the world over. Now the De Havilland Chipmunk is not a glider. It is not designed to be a glider. But one such day we found ourselves caught in this updraft. Even with the aircraft's nose pointing well below the horizon and the engine throttled back, our dear little aircraft with two excited people on board soared upwards at several hundred feet per minute - without engine power. This was another reminder of

Terence Horsley, who discovered 'standing waves' over the Grampian Mountains when his wartime aircraft was swept upward by such an updraft, unexplained in those days, but described in his book, *Soaring Flight,* of 1944. Eventually we dropped a wing and banked away, out of the updraft, and resumed normal powered flight over Loch Lomond. It did remind me how the airman and the salmon share similar dynamics of 'fluid in motion', utilising the currents of either air or water, to make their way in the world.

Concern on the Endrick

One of my first fishing outings from Glasgow was a late-autumn visit to the Pots of Gartness on the River Endrick, the main tributary of Loch Lomond. The sight was heartbreaking with the river and its banks littered with the bodies of dead and dying salmon, all covered in the white fungus linked to Ulcerative Dermal Necrosis (UDN). This disease had been decimating Scottish salmon stocks throughout the 1960s and was widespread. I was so affected that I wrote my first article: *At The End Of The Season* for *Rod and Line* magazine.

"It was my last day of the 1969 salmon fishing season on the River Endrick, Stirlingshire. The river was down again after a spate which had brought a fair stock of autumn fish upstream. It was a grey day. Low cloud scudded across the sky on a cold northerly breeze, throwing handfuls of sharp rain on the water. A squally wind was blasting the tired trees and the river was full of fallen leaves. I hadn't caught anything in the first pool, but hopes were still high as I moved downstream to the second until I saw the first corpse. It was lying in about a foot of peaty water, belly up, in a quiet backwater, a pale ghostly shape of what had been a fine salmon. I hadn't gone much further before I found another - and another. All along the river the banks were lined with dead fish.

Many, like the first, were in the water, others left high on the grass as the flood went down. They were all fine salmon. They lay now, red swollen corpses with the fungus of Ulcerative Dermal Necrosis (UDN) scarring their flanks like lichen on a dead tree. The crows had picked the eyes and the gulls and rats had feasted on the pale putrefying flesh until, of some, only the skeleton and scraps of skin remained. So this was the fate of the fine autumn run of fish that had left the loch and leapt the Pots of Gartness last week. I forced myself to continue fishing. But I had no enthusiasm for catching whatever mutilated monster I might tempt to a fly. Might there still be some clean fish in the water, a sea trout perhaps? And what about next year? Would there be any salmon next year?

I wandered downstream, making desultory casts as I went. Curtains of rain swept down the valley and the cloud lowered as mist on the surrounding hills. Flocks of fieldfares and redwings were being tossed southwards and fluttered for shelter in the swaying trees. I was wading a shallow riffle, when I almost stood on a fish. The water erupted in spray and noise as she torpedoed across the shallows and down into the pool. She was a salmon of about 10 lb in weight. Another dying fish struggling in the shallows I thought, until I noticed the patch of pale gravel. I went back upstream for half an hour and when I returned she was back again.

She was lying a little upstream of the pale patch of gravel and completely covered by the water. She was a fine hen fish, broad and deep and black with being so long in fresh water. She was well-camouflaged, except for her head, which was white with fungus She lay there, motionless, for a long time, just maintaining herself against the current. Occasionally, she would lose the struggle and drift downstream, only to thrash her way back to her station. I saw the cock fish leave the pool but I didn't see him cross the shallows until he was beside her. He was much smaller, barely 5 pounds, red and gold he looked, and he was clean.

As soon as he arrived she started spawning and he flashed his golden flanks as he lay on his side to fertilise the spawn. They moved off the redd for a short while and then returned to spawn again. Four times she spawned and four times the golden flanks of the cock fish showed. After each spawning she drifted further downstream and each time she thrashed her way back again. The fourth time she didn't make it. She drifted on down the pool and was lost to view. Soon she too would join the ranks of red, swollen corpses on the river bank, but she had survived long enough. Perhaps, some of her offspring will one day return to the river - clean".

13. NIGHTS IN GALLOWAY

"At 3000 feet the night is dark. Clear, but dark - very dark. We had passed the lights of Dumfries 10 minutes ago, Thornhill is on our left, Sanquhar is a trickle of lights up ahead. The few cars below on the A76, heading north, are travelling faster than we are. With our airspeed of only 90 knots against a headwind of 50 knots, we are making only 40 knots - some 45 mph. The few cars on the road below are overtaking us. Beyond Sanquhar is blackness as the moors of east Ayrshire stretch into the distance."

We had left Glasgow Airport early enough on a brisk January day. We were delivering a Chipmunk, a student and I, to RAF Woodvale, near Southport, for servicing and collecting another one to bring back to Glasgow. It was a lovely clear winter day with a northerly airflow down from the Arctic. We fairly flew down with a tailwind in 1 hr 30 min. We knew it would take longer to return to Glasgow against the headwind but there was also a delay with the aircraft we were taking back.

By the time we took off it was getting dark and the headwind was stronger. We struggled up the coast of the Lake District dragging past Sellafield and I decided to divert to Carlisle to top-up our fuel. It was just before 5 pm and Carlisle was about close down but agreed to stay open just for us. We landed in the dark, remembered how to do our own refuel and turnaround and got airborne again as quickly as possible. We skirted the Solway and were now punching our way slowly up the Nith valley, where lots of big 'greyback' salmon had run upriver last autumn.

Not far off to the west, hidden in the dark, but a forbidding presence on my flight map, loomed the high mountains of Galloway. Rising to over 2700 feet in the Merrick and a lonely desolate place, it was definitely somewhere to avoid in a small plane on a dark night. But there were to be many adventures on future dark nights in Galloway, on the ground and on its rivers.

Much later, a family holiday in Wigtown provided an opportunity to try for sea trout in the Water of Fleet:

"It is July and the night is going to be dark. A permit from the Murray Arms Hotel in Gatehouse of Fleet starts the ball rolling. Where is the most likely place? "The Bridge Pool", is the reply. A reconnaissance is required. We find the Bridge Pool, check the access, check the river bank, find a sand spit to stand on later and retire to the aforesaid Murray Arms Hotel for refreshments and sustenance. We return to the Bridge Pool. The night is definitely dark. The river bank all looks different. David goes downstream. I hog the Bridge Pool and wait. Gradually the eyes adjust to the shape of the far bank and the curves of the current. The ears get used to the rustles and scratches and plops of the night-time river. Suddenly there is a mighty crash at the bottom of the pool. A big fish - but is it a salmon or a sea trout? It doesn't matter, it is a big fish. My Stoat's Tail fishes the head of the pool quietly, no splashes, no excitement.

Time passes. Then, in one of those moments when the 'crack' appears, the familiar reality of the angler and his river slips into another dimension. The river noises fade out. The birds, bats, insects and other beasties go still. There is a primordial sensation that something wild is about to connect. It initially comes as a hesitation of the smooth drift of the line and fly. It is not the firm 'draw' of a salmon take. It is not the 'rugg! rugg!' of a small sea trout. It is as if the fly has gently snagged on the bottom and the current is curving the line downstream - just a gentle resistance. An ever-so-faint electric charge seems to come up the line and down the rod to the finger on the line just above the reel. Something is there!

I don't think I 'strike' or ever set the hook. The fish does that all by itself but suddenly all chaos breaks loose. The fish takes off down the pool, the reel screams and line disappears. Somewhere at the end of its run at the bottom of the pool it crashes upwards and sends a minor tsunami across the shallows. Then it is all over the place. I am not in control. The fish goes downstream, upstream and across-stream. To be fair it does not cheat. There is no head-shaking, no tail strumming and no snagging around rocks. It is just a fair tussle between a strong and clever fish and a duffer angler bungling around in the darkness of a strange pool in a strange river. No contest then! Somehow or other it begins to weaken and is more biddable to come towards the sand spit. I still have no idea what it is - a grilse, a big sea trout or a proper salmon? Whatever it is - is big. Now comes the crunch. In my arrogance I had made a deal with all my fish. If I could not land it without a net then it deserved to get away. So I have no net. I have no torch and it was so dark I could hardly see what was going on.

Enter the cavalry over the horizon. Okay, it is not the cavalry, only David. However, the cavalry has a landing net - a salmon-sized landing net. I have no idea to this day whether David heard my be-laboured huffs and puffs and, no doubt, oaths in the darkness or whether he had, through extra-sensory perception, sensed my need - but he arrives in the nick of time. By the time the landing net is deployed a large silver fish is ready to be coaxed into it, carried up the bank and despatched with a priest. It does not take us long to have a committee meeting and decide it is a sea trout - a fine specimen of a sea trout which is ceremoniously taken home to our cottage and weighed and photographed next day. A cock sea trout - 6 lb plus or minus an ounce or two."

All that was much in the future. Tonight we are still making slow progress up the valley of the Nith and there is a very vulnerable sensation crawling slowly north across the black moors of Ayrshire with no lights for miles in an elderly single-engined aircraft just out of major servicing. There is no place for a forced landing here if the engine misbehaves. Eventually the glow from Glasgow lights up the northern horizon and we make radio contact with Glasgow Airport. It took us 2 hr 45 mins airborne time for the journey home, including 1 hr 15 min night-flying. Just as well we had refuelled at Carlisle. A relieved Squadron Commander welcomed us home at Glasgow. I hadn't taken a torch as we had expected to be back in daylight!

14. 'GET-HOME-ITIS'

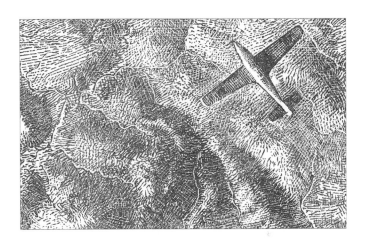

The salmon runs a few risks on its homing run back to its birthplace. It has to run the gauntlet of dolphins and seals in the estuary. It has to batter itself at almost impossible falls on its way upriver, never mind avoiding the odd otter and angler. It has to risk drought and flood without any advance forecasting. The salmon is obviously pretty determined to get home. So pilots can perhaps be forgiven for showing a similar determination to find their way home as well.

The salmon may have many diseases when it returns to freshwater but for pilots, the desire to get home causes a dangerous and all-consuming affliction crudely referred to as 'Get-Home-Itis.' The symptoms of this disease are common and easy to recognise. There are signs of rushing the preflight checks - because "we have done them so often and they are always OK". There is a tendency to accept aircraft of doubtful serviceability - on the basis that "we will get it fixed when we get back to base". And there is the temptation to interpret the weather forecast on the optimistic basis that - "they always err on the gloomy side so we can't blame them when it all goes pear-shaped".

Flying Chipmunks to and from Summer Camps in the south of England were always 'adventures'.

"We are on our way home. Four Chipmunks are in loose formation somewhere over the Cotswolds, heading for Church Fenton in Yorkshire to refuel before going home to Scotland. The weather forecast is reasonable but not great. But we are going home, aren't we? We are flying close enough to keep each other in sight without having to spend too much effort keeping position. We are far enough apart to provide 'lookout' cover for the formation as a whole and to keep a broad idea of where we are by map-reading the ground below. That proved to be quite useful.

Chipmunks - in transit

Twenty minutes after take-off I am struggling to match the features we are flying over with the map on my knee. We are not where we ought to be. Questions arise? Thirty seconds later comes the radio call from the lead aircraft : "Number 2, you have the lead I think my compass is unserviceable. We are a bit south of track". Thank you, Lead, I think!. Where the h*** are we? A disused airfield is identified. We aren't lost, 'just temporarily uncertain of our position'. The forecast had not been great for Church Fenton - 1000 foot cloud base, two miles visibility - should be within limits, but en-route is worse. The cloud is lowering and the pollution from industrial Midlands is reducing visibility. Not far ahead in the gloom are the Daventry masts, the highest and most significant obstruction to air traffic in that part of England. Some detailed track adjustments get us past that problem without actually seeing them in the haze.

Next problem - where is Church Fenton? A quick radio call will get us a 'steer', won't it? Well, it would have if they had answered - but silence. Try again. No reply. This was not unusual with our ten-channel VHF radio set. Not every station listened out on our frequencies - despite advance notice. The cloud is getting lower, the haze is getting thicker and we are getting low on fuel. Ouch! We were getting 'nibbled to death by ducks' - lots of little problems all leading up to an emergency. But help is at hand. Looming out of the gloom rises one of the huge cooling towers on the electricity generating stations which sprinkle the valleys of the Trent and the Aire. Excellent - but which one? There are several in this part of England. But at last we had a 'feature', so we set up in line-astern formation. Four Chipmunks orbiting this cooling tower at 800 feet must have interested the local population but no matter.

With no radio contact with Church Fenton it is time to swallow our pride and call the Emergency Frequency of 121.5 on VHF. With profound relief they reply immediately, triangulate us at Ferrybridge Power Station, give us a heading for Church Fenton and bring Church Fenton Air Traffic Control up on the Emergency channel. With a straight-in approach four Chipmunks and four relieved pilots land safely after more than 2 hours in the air. *"I learned about flying from that!"*

We waited until the weather improved before heading off 'homing' again - giving some credit to the skill and determination of the salmon.

Canberras can also have problems with 'get-home-itis':

"The tailplane of the aircraft in front seems to fill my windscreen. I watch its tail-light closely. It is close - but not too close! In the growing dark I just make out the whole shape of the other aircraft ahead against a paler night sky, an aircraft-shaped hole in the blanket of stars. We are on our way home. Two Canberra ex-bombers are somewhere over France at 30-odd thousand feet on our way back to Norfolk from Sardinia Only all is not going well!

Firstly, the weather briefing has somehow got 'lost in translation'. Decimomannu airbase in Sardinia was used by many NATO air forces but was managed by the Italian Air Force. The arrival forecast for the time we are due to arrive in Norfolk is unclear at best and not made any clearer by the 'translation'. A deep depression is approaching the UK with low cloud and high winds. It will arrive after we have landed safely back at base - we are told.

Secondly, our take-off was delayed. One of the aircraft was unserviceable and had to be fixed. My aircraft was to be the 'lead'. The detachment commander was in the other aircraft - and time was passing. By the time we were ready to set off, we were going to arrive later than forecast and well into the night. This would not normally be a problem - but the weather might be!

Thirdly, we are now well over France, in the dark with two problem aircraft. The navigation aids in my aircraft have failed and we have a long way to go across the busy airspace of France, now at night. I have now handed the 'lead' to the other aircraft and I am trying my best to fly formation at night - not often practised! Hence, I am sitting in comfortable line-astern with the lead aircraft outlined against a paler sky as we headed north.

But the aircraft I am following also has problems. In the rush to get airborne - 'get-home-itis' - the aircraft's belly tank has not been refilled with fuel by the ground crew. In the rush to get home this has not been checked by the aircrew. The aircraft in front now carries insufficient fuel to attempt to land at base and still have enough fuel to divert somewhere else. Our own aircraft has enough fuel to attempt a landing at base and still divert to another airfield if necessary. The only UK airfield with clear weather is RAF Valley in Anglesey - a long way from Norfolk and with a forecast for high winds.

We cruise north in the dark with occasional UK weather updates from French Air Traffic Control. The weather at the RAF bases in Germany is clear, so there is still an option to go there, but the weather at our base is deteriorating. By the time we make radio contact with the UK, decisions have been made. Once my aircraft has been handed over to UK radars and needs no further navigational assistance, the lead aircraft will divert straight to Valley. We will attempt to land at base and, if unsuccessful, will also divert to Valley. In the end we manage to land at base in a 50-knot wind which fortunately is blowing straight down the runway. We have a very short landing run and have to taxi all the way down the rest of the 6000 feet of tarmac to the end. Because of the strength of the wind, the aircraft cannot be turned off the runway across the wind so we have to be towed ignominiously, but gratefully, back to dispersal.

And what about Number 2. They got to Valley eventually but the wind when they arrived was outside crosswind limits for the Canberra on its main runway. Some tense minutes were experienced while they got the short secondary runway into use and a relieved crew landed safely - and wiser - with still some fuel on board."

15. 'FIND, FIX AND STRIKE' - AND FISH

From 30,000 feet the distant Hebrides are covered in cloud - thick cloud. Tops are around 15000 feet and the base is reported at 1000 feet, in heavy rain. True to form, we break cloud at 800 feet and come to a squelchy stop on Stornoway's short, bumpy and very wet runway. Not a very promising arrival. It is 1976. We are taking part in a large NATO exercise and six Canberras are detached to the Hebrides to provide an attack force to 'Find, Fix and Strike' assorted NATO navies.

Early morning take-offs sent four-aircraft formations to attack the nuclear-powered aircraft carrier USS Nimitz, somewhere off the north of Norway. Single 'intruder' missions found the Ark Royal - eventually. Since the Canberra had no radar or sophisticated electronics it is amazing how a big aircraft carrier like 'The Ark' can get lost in an even bigger North Sea. I developed instant admiration for the skills of Terence Horsley and the crews of the unsophisticated Swordfish aircraft (Stringbags) flown by the Fleet Air Arm during the Second World War. Their exploits and challenges in attacking the German fleet are graphically described in Horsley's book *Find, Fix and Strike* of 1943.

When we were not flying. there was time to relax and there is plenty of space in a Canberra for a fishing rod and other kit. One of the local RAF detachment knew all about the fishing and took one or two of us off into that huge expanse of moorland that fills the centre of the island of Lewis.

Lewis - "that huge bowl of peatland, lochs and sky…"

I don't know which of the many lochs he took us to but names don't matter. Just the sheer experience of being in the middle of that huge bowl of peatland, lochs and sky on a clear September day with the blue mountains of Harris filling the southern horizon was a moving experience and, as if on cue to complete the dream, high above us circled the massive wings of a golden eagle. It was an angler's paradise. Success came on other evenings, closer to Stornoway, just off the main road - small, dark, peaty lochans; eager trout - dark, golden and tasty.

I had first been tempted to fish the Hebrides by Negley Farson in his classic of fishing literature, *Going Fishing,* published in 1947. In the 1930's, Farson had regularly travelled by steamer to the Western Isles and his book has wonderful stories about Harris, Benbecula and the Uists. One September he fished in the three lochs above Tarbert in Harris, with "the prince of all gillies", Murdo Macdermid, "the perfect companion". It was here on his last day and his last hour that he was hooked into a reluctant salmon when the steamer was sounding its klaxon - "like a dying man"- preparing to depart. He just got on board as the steamer was casting off. Later, the Captain came to berate him but when he saw the fish he grinned and agreed "Well...perhaps it was worth waiting for that one." To get to Benbecula in those days he had to cross the sands and the shallow rip-tide in a horse and cart. "And the green waters of the Atlantic raced through our strong wheels up above the hubs."

Times have changed but there are still plenty lochs of all descriptions in the Western Isles. Most of the lochs are dark and peaty carved out of the ancient Lewisian gneiss rocks but where the geology changes there are spectacular differences. One of those differences is seen along the Atlantic coast of South Uist and Benbecula. Between there and America there is nothing but water and wind. Over the millennia the waves have ground down the cockles and scallops and the wind has built them up into a long, flat strip of fertile soil known locally as the 'machair'. This machair stretches, in one form or another, up the western seaboard but its best development is in South Uist and Benbecula, where it is studded with lochs which are home to specimen trout. The machair lochs are now considered to be an aquatic habitat of European importance and are designated as a European Union Special Area of Conservation. On South Uist the sea trout and salmon fishing is mainly on the more acid lochs, such as Roag and Fada, while the more alkaline lochs like Stilligary and Grogarry produce beautiful brown trout.

Following a community buy-out in 2006, the fishing on the machair lochs is now owned by Storas Uibhist. The South Uist Angling Club (SUAC) manages those lochs which are not reserved to Storas Uibhist, together with all the lochs across the causeway on Benbecula. Readily accessible lochs include West Loch Olavat and East Loch Olavat on Benbecula; and East Loch Bi, Loch an Duin Mhoir and Loch A'Phuirt-ruaidh (Fraser's Loch) on South Uist. Sea trout can also be taken from Strome and Bayhead lochs on a SUAC permit. On Benbecula, there are so many lochs to choose from that, if you are not catching fish, local wisdom advises: "Don't bother to change your fly, just change your loch."

A 10 lb sea trout about to be returned to Fada

16. ATTACKING THE ORKNEYS

One of our main exercises from Stornoway was to provide realistic low-level 'intruder' missions against the Royal Navy based in Scapa Flow.

"It is early on a clear September morning. The sun is just spreading its weak light across the eastern sky. We are sneaking in at very low level from the south-west, hidden from the fleet's radar behind the dark hump of the island of Hoy. Hopefully, we will surprise the ships of the Royal Navy, and other NATO navies, anchored in Scapa Flow. We may not be a surprise, however! We may have been spotted long ago by an anti-aircraft 'picket' ship before we got anywhere near Hoy and despatched with a sea-to-air missile. We do not know at this stage in the exercise. We crest the broad summit of Hoy and are faced with multiple ships anchored in Scapa. We choose one dark target outlined on the pale water and overfly it, clear of its masts and communications antennae, simulating our attack. Bomb gone! Fortunately for us, this time, we see no red tracer rounds curving towards us from anti-aircraft guns and no smoke from Seacat missiles following our exhausts. Our undoubted demise is recorded on some computer screen deep in the bowels of a ship. We will hear our inevitable fate eventually at debrief. "

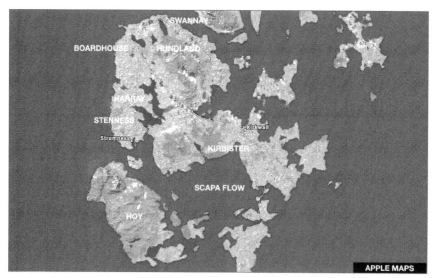

Orkney and its trout lochs - and Scapa Flow

I did not get to fish Orkney until 1982. Orkney amply demonstrates that "there is more to fishing than catching fish". Trout are only one of the pleasures of Loch Harray.

"We are fishing in a canvas of blue water, blue sky, white cloud, white skerries, green fields and brown moorland. Behind us rise the great Neolithic stone circle of the Ring of Brodgar. At the south end of the loch are the other great Standing Stones of Stenness and the unique prehistoric burial site of Maeshowe. Above and around us are myriads of birds. Gulls and terns are commonplace, in numbers. Curlew, redshank, oyster-catcher, sandpiper fill the air with sound. So trout are almost incidental."

Like Caithness, the Orkney Islands are built upon the rich flagstones of the Old Red Sandstone era. There are five main fishing lochs on Orkney Mainland – Harray, Boardland, Swannay, Hundland and Kirbister. These are all managed by the Orkney Trout Fishing Association (OTFA).

Loch Harray is the largest of the lochs and is separated from its tidal neighbour, Loch Stenness, by the culverts at Brodgar Bridge. It covers a windswept 1500 acres surrounded by the neat, dyked hayfields and the rolling moorlands of Orkney Mainland. Harray is widely regarded as the jewel in the Orkney trout fishing crown and the most famous fishery. The loch features large areas of productive skerries, shallows, bays and points, and with over 14 miles of shoreline it is probably the most popular of Orkney's wading loch especially in the earlier part of the season. As the season progresses and the water temperature increases then the fish move out into deeper, cooler, water when boat fishing comes into its own. Its clear water supports a rich food supply of caddis and mayfly species but, more particularly, large populations of shrimps and snails which give the deep red colour to the flesh of the trout.

The trout themselves are magnificent fish. More like sea-trout than brown trout they are silver in colour with a profuse covering of black markings and a deep red flesh which is excellent eating. The trout average around twelve ounces but fish over three pounds are fairly common The record stands at seventeen-and-a-half pounds from the 1960's. Tactics for fishing Harray are wide and varied and can change very quickly with the trout changing their feeding habits to capitalise on the most prolific food item of that particular day. No two days are the same. The food items most important and most likely to encourage the trout to feed avidly are the chironomid (midge, buzzer), caenis, cow-dung, daphnia, olive and snails. Of these, the midge can provide the most spectacular rises of fish. During these periods fish can be taken in large numbers so OTFA encourages anglers to show due restraint.

Other lochs in Orkney include the peat-stained waters of *Swannay*, the most northerly of the mainland lochs. This holds some of the highest quality trout in the county. It is probably the most enigmatic of the lochs with long periods of inactivity making it very dour but on its day it can provide spectacular sport.

Boardhouse tends to be the preferred loch of the visiting angler due mainly to the fact that it is virtually free of skerries and fish can be taken all over with long drifts across the middle of the loch often being the most productive. Wading can be successful at times usually in early season when fish are more likely to be feeding on the stones. The trout in the loch tend to average about 11-14 oz. with a two-pounder worthy of note. Weed growth from mid-summer onwards can reduce fishable areas but it seldom causes a problem.

Hundland is another peat-stained water which abounds with hidden skerries which can be difficult to spot, so caution is advised. The shallow nature of the loch makes it susceptible to fishing pressure but it can sometimes fish very well in bright sunshine. Wading the skerries can be productive but it is best tackled from a boat.

Kirbister is full of free-rising trout and is regarded as a splendid loch for those new to the sport and is very popular with junior anglers. Wading is easy and large baskets can be taken from the first day of the season to the last.

Stenness is the least-fished of the main Orkney lochs probably because it is most difficult to come to terms with. Its tidal nature causes wide fluctuations in water height and salinity in the loch, both of which have a marked affect on the resident trout population. The fish tend to feed in very shallow water and wading can be very good. The trout range from an average of 8-10oz to specimen 'yellowbelly' in excess of 4 lb. Following high tides, sea trout in the 1-2 lb category can be caught.

In the same year that I discovered the fishing on Orkney, the Royal Navy was defending itself in the Falklands Islands against the Canberras and Skyhawks of the Fuerza Aerea Argentina. On 1 May 1982, six Argentine Canberras approached the islands at very low level from the north-west, en-route to the San Carlos beachhead, but were picked up on a ship's radar. One was shot down by a Sea Harrier and the others retreated. The Canberras were eventually confined to night bombing missions against the beachhead and Mount Kent. It is hoped that some of our simulated attacks on the fleet at Scapa Flow in 1976 may have helped - just a little bit.

17. TROUT FROM THE TAPWATERS

From the right-hand seat of the Bulldog trainer, while the student is doing his good lookout, I can glance down at a small reservoir in the middle of the Pentland Hills and wonder if it contains trout. Further down the steep-sided valley another reservoir glints in the sun. Behind us, we have just crossed two other reservoirs above Balerno. Off to the west lies the vast windswept expanse of Harperrig and up ahead, on the other side of the Pentlands, gleams Gladhouse.

I was flying from the Royal Air Force station at Turnhouse, just outside Edinburgh, a station with a long and illustrious pedigree. A grass airfield was opened here in 1915 for the Royal Flying Corps. No 603 (City of Edinburgh) Squadron, Auxiliary Air Force, was formed in 1925 and Turnhouse was the most northerly air defence base in the United Kingdom. It was from here, on 16 October 1939, that No 603 Squadron shot down the first enemy aircraft of the Second World War. During an attack on the Port of Rosyth and the ships - HMS Repulse, HMS Southhampton and HMS Edinburgh - No 603 Squadron shot down a Heinkel 111 and Junkers JU88.

A Bulldog Trainer

Turnhouse, most importantly, proved to be in the middle of trout-fishing country. All of these reservoirs are full of wild brown trout and are a cornucopia for the fisherman. Within a few miles of Princes Street, trout anglers had a wide choice of trout fishing from Scotland's capital city.

"Gardyloo"

Edinburgh's public water supply did not start with reservoirs. In 1676 the Town Council paid a Dutch engineer, Peter Bruschi, the sum of £2950 Scots, to bring a supply of water from the Comiston Springs, three miles south of the city. The water was led down the hill into Edinburgh's Old Town, where young lads and lassies – the 'water caddies', delivered it from the public wells in the High Street to the top of the tenements at a charge of 1/2 p per barrel. The subsequent waste-water, with all its contents, was later despatched from the same tenements, out the window, to the warning of 'Gardyloo" - a corruption of the

French 'Garde de l'eau!' - which echoed down the narrow and unhygienic 'closes' of the Old Town. It was not until 1822 that Thomas Telford and Robert Jardine built Edinburgh's first decent-sized reservoir at Glencorse, in the Pentland Hills. Other reservoirs were built to meet the expanding needs of a growing population and are described in detail in the book *Trout Reservoirs of Lothian: 1976 -1996.*

The 400-acre Gladhouse Reservoir is considered the 'Jewel in the Crown' of the Edinburgh reservoirs. It lies against the magnificent backdrop of the Moorfoot escarpment and is a classic brown trout water with a big reputation, both locally and nationally - famed for first-class, top-of-the-water brown trout fishing. The late Bill Currie, who fished Gladhouse every Tuesday for many years, reckoned that: "Gladhouse ... keeps reminding me that whatever I know about fishing, it is only a tiny proportion of what there is to know. Gladhouse is thus a type of archetype, it keeps its secrets well."

A pilot's view of Gladhouse

Apart from fishing, we also did our share of flying. One memorable flight on 12 January 1978 was from Turnhouse to Kemble, with Alastair, to deliver one Bulldog and collect another.

"By 9am we are airborne, in a clear blue sky, heading south across the Pentlands towards the Tweedsmuir Hills. The Bulldog cruises at 120 knots and with a strong northerly tailwind we make excellent time. We cross the Solway at Annan, follow salmon rivers up the Eden and down the Lune. The Forest of Bowland is on the left and we find our way through industrial Lancashire. There is always a messy area of uncertain landmarks and poor visibility in the gap between Liverpool and Manchester, underneath the airways and around the Manchester Control Area. But we are through that and soon pick up the Severn, find the Cotswolds and land at Kemble after only 1hr 45m. The way back north was a different story. Punching against, what was now, a very strong headwind it took us 3 hours flying time plus a refuelling stop at Woodvale. We got back in daylight and in time for tea."

Kemble at that time was the home of the Royal Air Force 'Red Arrows' Aerobatic Team and we had a chance to see the red-painted Folland Gnats in dispersal. Whether that inspired Alastair or not, I could not say, but Alastair subsequently joined the RAF and eventually became leader of the Red Arrows Aerobatic Team. Serendipity!

RAF Turnhouse was a 'homing' for me - like the salmon. I had first come to Turnhouse in my youth as an avid aircraft spotter on 'Battle of Britain' Open days. The sights and sounds of the aircraft were imprinted in those days - so perhaps Turnhouse might be considered as my 'natal stream'. My days as a military aviator were coming to a close. Anticipating leaving the Royal Air Force, I had obtained my Private Pilot's Licence and managed to afford a few flights in private aircraft.

My swansong was a 1 hr 30 min flight in a Grumman to see the territory of my new Lothian Regional Council career from the air. In clear conditions, I flew up the west side of the Pentlands, past Harperrig and Crosswood reservoirs, to Carstairs, up the Clyde to Lamington. At Biggar I turned east, over to the upper Tweed and flew downstream, over Stobo and Bemersyde as far as Coldstream then turned north up to the Whiteadder and Hopes reservoirs. Little did I realise then how large a part the River Tweed would play in my later life. Abeam the Hopes Reservoir, I climbed to 10,000 feet, circling like a buzzard, and had my last view of Scotland as pilot-in-command. This stretched from the Cheviot to the Tay, from the North Sea to the Ochils, with the Lammermuirs and Moorfoots in the foreground and the dark shapes of the Pentland Hills to the west. A foretaste of my next career and my future involvement with the Clyde, the Tweed and the Edinburgh reservoirs. But that was all in the unknown future.

Farewell to the Royal Air Force

18. 'THE LITTLE RIVER'

The River South Ask in Angus was Terence Horsley's 'Little River'. "The little river", he recalls, "rises among mountains as remote and as rugged as those of the big river. Its birth is a gush from the loins of a royal peak and, after rain, it is as bright as a gleaming sword". Then speaking as a pilot, he describes the challenge of flying a small plane down these windswept mountains: "I have pried upon its beginnings through the windows of my plane, sliding down the crusted brow of its mother mountain while she has buffeted me with her gasping breath - so that I have been compelled to slap the control column from side to side to remain on an even keel. Then with bank and rudder, and a throttled engine, I have dropped like a plummet into the gloomy nursery of its young life."

More prosaically, the South Esk starts life in the high hills of the Grampians and after traversing Glen Clova, emerges into the great sandstone lowland of Strathmore and on into the North Sea through Montrose Basin. On its way it drains some of the richest farmland in Scotland and passes through the ancient and historic burghs of Kirriemuir, Brechin and Montrose. It also contains such evocative salmon and sea trout fishings as Cortachy Castle, Downie Park, Inshewan, Tannadyce, Justinhaugh, Finavon and Kinnaird.

The South Esk

My own interest in the South Esk? Well, both flying and fishing! I first looked down on the river from my Chipmunk aircraft on my first navigation exercise from Scone, to Kirriemuir to Brechin and back to base. From the air it looked attractive and I vowed I would return. In my subsequent twenty years of flying, I had, like Horsley, "lingered in the sunlight above the peaks of the Cairngorms and marvelled at the apparent innocence of the land". And yet again, like Horsley, I had "flown southwards at four miles to every minute....until the ground split and the headwaters of the South Esk were suddenly below."

In 1941 Horsley was the tenant on Finavon. During that time he applied his analytical skills as a pilot to the experiences of salmon fishing. In his book, *Fishing for Salmon and Trout*, published in 1947, he provided one of the first empirical records to show the relationship between salmon catches and river height, where all his catches in that month occurred on a falling water level. On the basis of his records for August 1941, he demonstrated that, on the 4th of the month, heavy showers brought the river up and his first salmon was caught on the 6th as the water level dropped. On the 12th heavy rain and a strong south-east wind started a series of spates with fish landed on falling water on the 14 and 18 . A further series of very heavy showers brought river up again from 26/27 and three salmon were caught on 28/29.

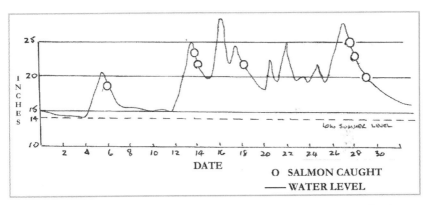

Finavon. August 1941: Salmon caught in relation to river levels

From Horsley's base at HMS Condor at Arbroath, the South Esk was just beyond the airfield circuit. He describes:

"During the minutes which my observer required to obtain wireless permission to "pancake", I could fly across the seven-hundred-foot ridge....inspect my water, noting whether there were poachers about....noting the height of the water by a stone on the edge of the pool, and discovering on the way a remarkable fund of information about the birds and beasts along the banks."

He had a love-hate relationship with his 'little river', as he called it. His first fish was a 20 lb Spring salmon and he caught many others, yet his river could be a fickle mistress. "Oh reluctant, horrid little river!" he wrote, "I wasted a gallon of petrol on you today, convinced that you would repay it. Do you remember that, when I flew over you this morning, you showed me your stone half uncovered and its shingle beach already partially clear. You had it hidden yesterday under your brown flood, but on your own reckoning you were today in perfect order. Deceptive wretch!"

It was many years before I could follow Horsley to his 'Little River' with a salmon rod in my hand - but I did eventually. I caught my first salmon in the Beech Tree Pool on, what was then called, the Shielhill beat. I was fishing from the right hand bank, let in those days by Kinnordie Estate. It was 7 October with a good height and colour to the water. As a beginner I had been persevering with fly-fishing, without success. A fellow-angler suggested that the conditions were more suitable to spinning which was still allowed in those days.

"I put up a black-and-gold Devon and spun it down the pool - once, twice - on the third cast the line stopped and I thought I had snagged the bottom. After a couple of tugs a large tail - a very large spade-like tail, appeared above the surface. I was transfixed. The line started to move slowly, majestically, down the pool and the rod bent. I suddenly tried to remember all the advice I had ever read about how to play a salmon - keep the rod up; give it line; keep the line tight; drop the rod-point when it jumps; get downstream of the fish; keep it out of shallow water; don't let it thrash on the surface - all the advice cramming through the brain as I try to keep control. No! Just contact will do - with an apparently large salmon. After an interminable time when I thought I had lost it once or twice, it tired and came in to the bank. Another crisis - my net was too small - a triangular folding thing for trout. By dint of more struggles and imagination the front part of the fish went into the net and the rest of it followed unceremoniously on to the bank where it was crudely bundled as far away as possible from any chance of flapping back into the river. It was not a big fish - only ten pounds or so in weight. It was not a pretty fish. It was a cock salmon getting on in spawning livery, with a fair bit of red on its skin and an impressive kype to its lower jaw. Nowadays it would go back but that day it was the most beautiful salmon in creation and my Stone Age alter-ego knocked it on the head and carried it triumphantly home to my cave, to be hailed as the successful hunter-gatherer."

There are moments in time when a crack appears. It may be a small crack or a large rent but from time-to-time such a crack appears and one is allowed to see into, and be in, another time. Such an occasion is the hooking of a first, or any other, salmon. The adrenaline rush, the heightened awareness, the intensity of focus, of anticipation of the prey's next move, takes one back far, far in time to the essential paradigm of predator and prey, hunter and quarry, to the deep inner part of our existence and folk-memory. One returns for those long minutes to a primitive hunter-gatherer, the small dark men of prehistory. By the time of the Picts the 'salmon of wisdom' was already part of their deep-time past. Pitting their wits against a powerful, fast and innovative animal - the salmon. The rest is history - "Those whom the Gods seek to destroy; they first allow to hook a salmon".

The South Esk is now recognized as a Special Area of Conservation (SAC) under the EU Habitats Directive because:

"The river supports a large, high-quality salmon population in a river draining a moderate-sized catchment on the east coast of Scotland.... The high proportion of the South Esk which is accessible to salmon and the range of ecological conditions in the river allows it to support the full range of life-history types found in Scotland, with sub-populations of spring, summer salmon and grilse all being present."

From 2004 to 2009 the South Esk was one of only eight Scottish salmon rivers forming the Conservation of Atlantic Salmon in Scotland (CASS) project, sharing EU money under the LIFE-Nature environmental programme. Practical activities undertaken by the Esk District Salmon Fishery Board included surveys of salmon habitat and juvenile numbers together with extensive fencing of river corridors in the upper catchment to control grazing, reduce erosion and prevent siltation of spawning gravels. One of the key activities of the CASS programme was raising awareness of salmon conservation. The 'Salmon in the Classroom' project introduces children to the wonders of salmon by hatching salmon eggs in schools and growing the resulting fry until they are old enough to release back into their local river. The River South Esk Catchment Management Plan was produced in 2008. A second catchment management plan, for the period 2020-24 will focus on the environment, people and economic opportunities.

19. THE BIG RIVER

It started as a distant growl, rose and faded as it did some turns and then came crashing and howling down the river at very low level. The peace was well and truly shattered. My fishing companion covered his ears and swore. I stopped fishing and gazed after the spot on the horizon where it had disappeared. It took me far away from the riverbank to a former and slightly less peaceful life - pure nostalgia. "A Tornado", I explained to my friend. "Bloody noisy!" was the stifled reply. I had hung up my flying gloves by the time I fished the Tweed. I had left the RAF - but the RAF had not left me.

Horsley's 'Big River' was the Tay. My 'Big River' was the Tweed. Not as big as the Tay but big enough. I was first charmed by the Tweed in William Scrope's classic book *Days and Nights of Salmon Fishing in the Tweed,* of 1843. Scrope was a great Tweed salmon fisher and pundit in the early part of the 19th century. This was still a time when legitimate salmon anglers had to compete with the ancient practice of 'leistering' for salmon with a multi-pronged salmon spear. His descriptions of Tweed salmon flies are fascinating, with names like 'Kinmont Willie', 'Meg with the Muckle Mouth' and 'Meg in her Braws'.

He also provided dubious advice about wading. "Never go into the water deeper than the fifth button of your waistcoat….", he warned, "And if you be wading in the month of February, when it may chance to freeze very hard, pull down your stockings, and examine your legs. Should they be black, or even purple. it might be as well to get on dry land; but if they are only rubicon, you may continue to enjoy the water." Needless to say, I purchased a set of good neoprene waders as soon as possible and despite such warnings Scrope got me started on serious salmon fishing on Tweed.

My very first visit to Tweed was to The Lees, above Coldstream, with Derek in the autumn of 1979, with a borrowed rod. We had the use of the boat on the Temple Pool and Derek hooked a beautiful 17 lb fish. I had to play boatman for the first time, to get us and the fish safely on the bank, but I was captivated. Over the years I have returned to Tweed many times, not always successfully, but spent many of those days on Bemersyde, where Thomas the Rhymer once predicted:

Tyde what may, whate'er betyde,
Haig shall be Haig of Bemersyde'.

Lord 'Dawyck' Haig of Bemersyde acceded to his title, 2nd Earl Haig, on the death of his father, Field Marshal Earl Haig, in 1928 and became laird of the eponymous estate and proprietor of one of the most fascinating salmon beats on Tweed. Since then, salmon and salmon fishing had been an important part of his life but not the only part. Lord Haig was a man of many parts – soldier, Colditz prisoner-of-war, acclaimed artist, landowner, indefatigable worker in the cause of ex-servicemen – as well as fishing proprietor, one-time Tweed

Commissioner and salmon angler. I had the privilege of interviewing Lord Haig in 2008 - the year before he died.

"I caught my first salmon, at the end of September 1928 at the tail of the Stream." Lord Haig confided. "It was an autumn fish, fairly fresh. The ghillie was Adam Rutherford, said to have been descended from the gypsies at Yetholm. He was a great storyteller and tended to exaggerate. He had taught me to fish for trout from the boat for a year or so. My mother was also present and she was delighted by my catch. My father had died in the January. The rod was a greenheart, far too heavy for me, very tiring". A first salmon, vividly remembered after 80 years.

Lord Haig had seen a few salmon run through Bemersyde - and a few changes - over the 80 years he had fished it and was delighted to share his experiences. Tall, spare and infinitely courteous, he talked to me in the study of his ancient Border keep, rebuilt in 1580, with his Norfolk terrier at his feet, and transported us back in time to a gentler, more elegant, less frenetic age between the two World Wars. Bemersyde salmon fishery could be briefly described as "one of the middle beats of Tweed" but this would be a gross understatement. Like a Maserati - is just a car! Bemersyde is more than just a salmon fishing. Its history goes 'away with the fairies' you could say. It is a holy place. It is one of the most secluded and spectacular parts of a spectacular river. And, almost as an extra, it also produces some 200 salmon each season.

Most people first see Bemersyde and the Eildon Hills from high up at Scott's View on the back road from Earlston to St Boswell's. This viewpoint was, of course, the favourite of the bard, Sir Walter Scott. Tradition has it that the horse pulling the cortege to his funeral at St Boswells involuntarily stopped at this spot - his favourite view. The view is rightly to be appreciated. From high above the river, the eye is immediately drawn to the three peaks of the Eildon Hills in the middle distance, the long sweep of the upper Tweed valley to the right and the distant hills around Tweedsmuir and Galloway on the horizon. Scott's View is perched above the 200-foot ancient river meander, called the Gateheugh - Tweed's answer to Symond's Yat on the Wye - carved down into deep layers of red sandstone strata. To the left the view leads down to the barrelling white waters at the top of the Halliwell Stream and the Boat Pool, just around the corner. To the right, the view runs upstream into the salmon beats of Ravenswood and Gledswood – tributes to the days gone by when the raven and the gled (kite) owned this valley.

Straight ahead, just across the river on the south bank of the river lies Old Melrose, the original site of Melrose Abbey, occupied by the Cistercian monks, before they moved upriver to another site at Melrose. This is hallowed ground. The Halliwell (Holy Well) Stream reflects the holy ground of the old abbey and the Monks Ford, where the holy ones crossed to Dryburgh Abbey, is just downstream of Woodside. Although no buildings remain at Old Melrose the sense of history and religious observance is strong and the monks and their sheep are never far away. "Where fair Tweed flows round holy Melrose and Eildon slopes to the plain."

The Eildons have another dark connection with Lord Haig and Bemersyde. Thomas Learmonth, laird of Ercildoune (Earlston) - also known as Thomas the Rhymer - was a famous poet and soothsayer of the 13th century. Tradition has it that he was so well in with the fairies that they abducted him and dragged him off into the bowels of the Eildon Hills, never to be seen again – at least by God-fearing Christian folk! Thomas, it was, who said the sooth that defines Bemersyde and the family of Haig: "Tyde what may, whate'er betyde, Haig shall be Haig of Bemersyde"

The Eildon Hills and Thomas' prophesy about the Haig succession provide a fitting introduction to Bemersyde, not only spectacularly scenic but steeped in history and providing a diversity of salmon-holding water and some excellent trout and grayling fishing. Bemersyde produces its annual bag of salmon from a very unusual and distinctive water with a number of famous and iconic pools and lies: - The Cromweil; The Dish; Boat Pool; Sangsters; Woodside. The origin of most of the names are lost in the mists of time but they all have their own stories.

Ian Farr has been boatman on Bemersyde for 32 years and knows every stone and lie in the river. There is no hiding place for salmon but each pool has its own season and height of water. At the top of Bemersyde, the Cromweil is a high-water beat, fishing best in the heavy waters of spring and autumn. The route to the 'Crom' is an adventure in itself. It starts at the Fishing Hut - the 'Operations Centre' - of Bemersyde. The boatman ferries you across the top of the Boat Pool in front of the Hut, in one of the two boats. A simple exercise, perhaps, except that, in high water on a dark November day, those of a classical bent might conjure up visions of another ferryman, Charon, rowing the 'newly dead' across the River Styx on the way to Hades, or the Underworld. But you end up safely, not in the Underworld, but on the hallowed ground of Old Melrose for a gentle stroll up the flat side of the Gateheugh (the Ravenswood side) to the Cromweil boat, which takes you across the river again to Bemersyde's left bank, below the Halidean Burn.

The 'Crom' at this point consists of a broad sandstone shelf stretching out some six metres from the bank, before dropping sharply into the depths of the pool, where the fish lie in layers at times on and under a series of shelves and ledges. Not far from the top of the Bemersyde part of the pool, a large rock splits the current at depth. There are three ways of fishing the 'Crom'. With the boatman at the oars he takes us gently down the shelf far enough out to cover the deeper water beyond the edge of the shelf. A cast, a drift, a cast, a drift and the 'Crom' is covered. When a fish is on Ian beaches the boat and you play it from the bank. When conditions suit, Ian can 'rope' the boat down the pool, letting out rope as the boat drifts downstream. If you are deemed to be fit to fish the 'Crom' on your own, there is an anchor in the boat which catches readily on the sandstone shelf and the rope wound figure-of-eight around the thole pins is let out like Granny's knitting, one loop at a time, dropping the boat another two metres downstream. While this is great fun, netting and boating a fresh and lively fish on your own from the boat is a challenge. At the tail of the 'Crom' the water shallows and the shelf breaks up into a series of blocks and pockets which often hide fish. This area, below the Oak Tree, can be fished from the bank. The fast water of the tail itself is the main route into the 'Crom' for fish which have fought their way up the Gateheugh and rest for a fatal minute or two.

The Cromweil flows into the Gateheugh, described by Sir Herbert Maxwell in *"The Story of the Tweed"* as "a wilder piece of fishing-water there is not in the whole river", and one that can be fished in a peculiar way. "The boatman, wading to his armpits, picks his way down the very centre of the torrent by secret shallows known only to the expert, holding the boat from which the angler casts his flies." There are four main lies in the Gateheugh – Upper Corbie, Lower Corbie, The Dish and Copper Beech. Without the boat, the Gateheugh is an interesting summer beat, with exciting wading for fish lying in surprisingly small pockets of fast water. The Copper Beech shallows down towards the Halliwell Stream and then down into the Boat Pool proper.

The 'Boat' is a great holding pool at most heights of water and can be fished from both the boat and both banks. Near the tail of the pool lie the Cradle and Cradle Rock. This is a collection of large rocks and ledges arranged in a cradle-shaped layout which provides a sheltered lie for fish which have just pushed up the fast water from Sangster's stream at the top of Woodside. Although there is a perfectly proper river gauge at the Boat Pool, measuring in boring old feet-and-inches, one of the charming quirks of Bemersyde is the traditional method of describing river levels in terms of 'tanks'. No-one can tell me when the tank, a common loft cold-water tank, appeared and lodged firmly on the right bank of the Stream opposite the Fishing Hut, but there it has stayed and over the years the river level has been described as either Below-tank, Quarter-tank, Half-tank, Top-tank or Above-tank. Not very scientific perhaps, so when the original tank disintegrated some ten years ago Ian satisfied tradition by replacing it with another attic tank but brought it into the modern age by painting actual measurements at 2-inch intervals upon it.

Woodside is the gentler side of Bemersyde. The stream at the head – Sangster's – is sometimes best fished from the far bank and holds a fish or two. It also holds spawning sea lampreys in season and you can waste an afternoon, as I did, casting hopefully to what appeared to be salmon showing with regularity! Below Sangster's, Woodside is a fairly broad, shallow and regular flow. To provide variety, three small groynes stick out from the left bank into the flow and provide deeper lies and shelter for travelling fish. It is easy walking. No need to wade but a Spey cast is a useful skill. Sometimes the best is kept to last. Right at the bottom of Woodside at the end of the Bemersyde water is Jock's Shore. Don't ask me where the name comes from. Nobody knows but Jocks Shore is a small cleft or crack in the sandstone slabs. Running fish find rest and shelter just above the fast water of Monk's Ford below.

My Record Book reminds me that I had my first visit to Bemersyde on 12 February 1982, when Eric Stevenson was boatman. I fished one day each month that season - and caught nothing, not even a kelt! In 1983 I caught a couple of kelts from the Boat Pool but it was 10 February 1984 before I caught my first proper Tweed salmon - a beautiful Spring fish of 14 lb from the Cromweil. My 10 visits in 1984 produced another two fish - 20 lb and 6 lb - from the Boat Pool on 16 November. In 1985 my 10 visits produced a matching pair of summer salmon on 7 June at 6 lb and 6.5 lb from The Dish. In 1986 I only landed one fish - a 14.5 lb 'Springer' on 14 February from the Boat Pool, in the company of Jack. We caught identical fish, both bars of silver at 14.5 lb, except that the one Jack caught was seal-damaged on one side. We laid them out side-by-side - good side up. A perfect pair. What a shame about Jack's fish! Jack left the river early, taking his fish with him, of course. But the one that was left was seal-damaged! At dusk on the 1 August 1986, I had three salmon of 8, 9.5 and 10.5 lb, from Boat Pool, Sangsters and The Stream respectively, all in quick succession (Perhaps on one of Horsley's 'falling' waters). In 1987 I had a 11.5 lb salmon from The Stream on 7 August and a sea trout of 8 lb from Jock's Shore on Woodside on 9 October. My last full season was 1990 - with no fish!

Big Fish

Big fish are not unknown from Bemersyde. Above the fireplace in Lord Haig's study is a cased specimen of 43 lb from the dim and distant past, but another of 42 lb was caught in 1987. These are dwarfed by the 64 lb salmon hooked and lost by Arthur Balfour Haig in the afternoon of 29 November 1883. In a signed statement he tells that: - In the company of his fisherman, Moody, and the under-fisherman, the fish was hooked in the Boat Pool and took them down through Woodside and Jock's Shore to the Monk's Ford at the top of Dryburgh:

"After nearly an hour's play the fish was tired out and the under-fisherman went into the water to net him - he had the fish's head three times in the net but each time it slipped out again. The man said the net would hold only the fish's head and that it was hopeless to try to get him with the net. After the third try the gut broke and the fish escaped. I heard afterwards that a noted poacher called Paterson assisted by others got the fish out the following night and they asserted that he weighed 64 lb."

The under-fisherman's name is not recorded!!

Bemersyde is a magical place. Apart from fairies and monks, generals and earls, salmon and the 'newly dead', there are other - unholy - things at Bemersyde. November seems to be the spooky time. A neighbour of Bemersyde, the late Lord Brackley (later Duke of Sutherland) and his sister saw the ghost of Arthur Balfour Haig riding his horse across the fields between Bemersyde and Dryburgh. Lord Haig told me of another ghost – a lady ancestor – who is said to haunt the Boat Pool. She fell in unrequited love with one of the monks of Old Melrose and ended it all by committing suicide in the river. The monk was sentenced to bathe every day throughout the year in penance for his fault. On a dark November night she is said to emerge from the waters of the Boat Pool, emit her other-worldly shriek and sink back below the surface. Having frequently been the last rod to leave the Boat Pool in the Stygian gloom of a November night, I have no difficulty in believing the story.

The Scottish Borders, during my visits, was virtually covered by a military Low Flying Area. The Tweed ran through the Scottish Borders and my days of fishing on Tweed provided a cavalcade of the developing aircraft types operated by the RAF over the years since I had left. The Canberras had already been superseded, in the RAF Germany strike role, by Buccaneers, F4 Phantoms, Jaguars and then by Tornadoes. Together with UK-based squadrons they came over for low flying training and NATO exercises. Harriers and Hawks, aircraft variety, were frequent attackers and the Tornado F3 interceptors from Leuchars mounted Combat Air Patrols overhead or pursued them at low level across the landscape. There were few days when fishing was not enlivened by the thunder of jet engines at high power and low level. For many of my fishing companions they were an intrusion, a noisy distraction from the peaceful enjoyment of the riverside. But for me they took me far away from the riverbank and I felt like Terence Horsley, watching the Hurricane with his friend on the bank of his chalk stream in 1940 - pure nostalgia.

20. LAST CAST WITH HORSLEY

It is a dark night …

I fish with Horsley for the last time - at Finavon. It is a dark night in June, not long after midsummer, and the only noise is the occasional splash of a sea trout. It should be a clear night, up here in the far north, but it is cloudy with a thick layer of strato-cumulus from 1000 feet to 10000 feet with poor visibility underneath. I am the only rod on the beat tonight, I think, and I am enjoying having the Milton Beat to myself until I see the dark shadow further down the Beeches Pool. He is quiet, knee deep at the pool-tail just the swish-swish of his rod betraying his presence.

"Long-time friend of the owner", he offers, sensing my surprise at the intrusion. There is plenty of room for both of us and the sea trout aren't taking yet. He seems a nice enough guy, polite and well-spoken in an old-fashioned sort of way. A traditionalist, I assume or even a collector, as I admire his classic split-cane rod. He doesn't have a Barbour jacket, just one of those retro, fleece-lined Air Force surplus things. "Used to be a tenant here, a long time back", he continues, "Just get the odd night off now and then, when the weather is too bad for flying". I wish him luck, leave him to it and move on down to the next pool.

The ghillie turns up later, to check my progress. I tell him I have met the other guest. "What other guest?" he asks. There is no other guest, he tells me. I describe the bomber jacket, split cane rod and old fashioned ways and recognition dawns. "This happened one night last year", he says. "Filthy night, too", he reminisces. "Strange chap. Never any bother. No idea who he is. Must like his sea trout fishing." Back at the hut, when we get there, laid out on the grass, is a brace of sea trout.

"A brace of sea trout....."

Pinned to the door, scribbled on a scrap of paper, is the message, "Thanks for the hospitality - "Stringbag". I turn it over. It is torn off an aeronautical chart, with airfields marked in purple. The bottom corner of the map, written in blue, reads "Fleet Air Arm, 1941".

AUTHOR

Drew Jamieson trained as a geographer. His first career spanned 20 years as a pilot and flying instructor in the Royal Air Force. His further career included fisheries management, conservation and environmental planning in local government and the water industry. His writings have been published in The Scotsman, The Scottish Field, The Atlantic Salmon Journal and other angling magazines. This is his eighth title published on Amazon.

OTHER TITLES IN THIS SERIES

"A Scottish Angler's Companions": "The author has met many people during a lifetime of angling but while most of us meet people, he befriends them and here remembers them fondly. Drew Jamieson .....shares that friendship with the reader in an easy to read manner.

"Where the Wild Trout Swim": "......written in a pleasant flowing language which is how all books should be written. I recommend it to all trout anglers but also to all lovers of the English language."

Tom McGregor, United Clyde Angling Improvement Association

"Trout from Scottish Reservoirs": "This is a fascinating read...... In many ways this book is a little gem, which provides both an historical account but also a reference for the management of trout reservoirs."

FISH Magazine, The Institute of Fisheries Management

"Where the Wild Salmon Run"; "A Scottish Angler's Companions": "Jamieson's writing evokes many different segments of the salmon's world.....He reaches far and wide to open a window on the history, culture, biology, science and joy of this wonderful wild animal. Jamieson's writing comes from the heart and it reveals a deep concern for the fish we love"

Atlantic Salmon Journal

"Where the Wild Trout Swim"; "Where the Wild Salmon Run"; "A Scottish Angler's Companions": "His careful observation of trout and salmon, his advice on managing reservoirs and the classic waters for anglers make these three books a great read. His charming boyhood tales and fishing experiences demonstrate his extensive knowledge."

Scottish Field

BOOKS WORTH READING

Brooke, Mike. (2012). *A Bucket of Sunshine.* The History Press, Stroud.

Brooke, Mike. (2013). *Follow Me Through.* The History Press, Stroud.

Crosbie, Harry H. (1993). *On a Wing and a Prayer.* HarperCollins, USA.

Currie, William.B. (1984). *Days and Nights of Game Fishing.* George Allen and Unwin, London.

Farson, Negley. (1947). *Going Fishing.* Country Life, London.

Horsley, Terence. (1943). *Find, Fix and Strike.* Eyre and Spottiswood, London.

Horsley, Terence. (1944). *Soaring Flight.* Eyre and Spottiswood, London.

Horsley, Terence. (1944). *Fishing for Trout and Salmon.* H.F. & G. Witherby, London.

Horsley, Terence. (1947). *Fishing and Flying.* Eyre and Spottiswood, London.

Horsley, Terence. (1947). *The Long Flight.* Country Life, London.

Horsley, Terence. (1947). *Sporting Pageant: A Gun, A Rifle, And An Aeroplane.* H.F.& G. Witherby, London

Jamieson, Drew. (2018). *A Scottish Angler's Companions.* Amazon.

Jamieson, Drew. (2019). *The Trout Reservoirs of Lothian.* Amazon.

Lamont, Henry. (1931). *Loch Lomond – A Study in Angling Conditions.* Jackson, Wylie and Co, Glasgow.

Lamont, Henry. (1932). *Days and Ways of a Scottish Angler.* Allan, London.

Maxwell, Sir Herbert. (1909). *The Story of the Tweed.* James Nisbet and Company, Limited, London.

Netboy, Anthony. (1968). *The Atlantic Salmon: A Vanishing Species.* Faber and Faber, London.

Reid, John. (1971). *Clyde Style Flies and Their Dressings.* David and Charles.

Scrope, William. (1843) *Days and Nights of Salmon Fishing in the Tweed.* John Murray, Edinburgh.

Sharp, Robert C. (1973). *Let's Fish the Clyde.* The Motherwell Times, Motherwell.

Spender, Stephen. (1955). *"The Truly Great",* from *Collected Poems 1928-1953.* Random House Inc.

Stewart, William C. (1857). *The Practical Angler; or The Art of Trout Fishing.* A. & C. Black, Edinburgh. (1905 edition Adam and Charles Black, London.)

Stoddart, Thomas Tod. (1866). *An Angler's Rambles and Angling Songs.* Edmonston and Douglas, Edinburgh.

Wood, Ian. (1957). *My Way with Salmon.* George Allan and Unwin, London.